Sailing in Dangerous Waters

A Director's Guide to Data Governance

E. Michael Power
Roland L. Trope

ABA Section of
BUSINESS LAW
Practical Resources for the Business Lawyer

Defending Liberty
Pursuing Justice

Printed in the United States of America.

Library of Congress Cataloging-in-Publication Data

Power, E. Michael.
Sailing in dangerous waters : a director's guide to data governance / by E. Michael Power and Roland L. Trope.
    p. cm.
Includes bibliographical references.
ISBN 1-59031-539-1 (hardcover)
    1. Corporate governance—Law and legislation—United States. 2. Databases—Law and legislation—United States. 3. Data protection—Law and legislation—United States. I. Trope, Roland L. II. Title.
KF1422.P69 2005
346.73′0664—dc22   2005010268

Discounts are available for books ordered in bulk. Special consideration is given to state and local bars, CLE programs, and other bar-related organizations. Inquire at Book Publishing, American Bar Association, 321 North Clark Street, Chicago, IL 60610.

10   09   08   07   06   05   5   4   3   2   1

We wish to thank our families, Cindy and Winston Trope, Peggy Domville, Conor and Nicholas Power, for their patience, love, and understanding while we consumed far too much of "their" time in preparing this book and practicing law.

Contents

Acknowledgements

During the preparation of this book, the authors received comments, insights, criticism, and suggestions from several colleagues and friends. Their contributions substantially improved the manuscript. We wish to express our gratitude to:

Kim Bath, Orrie Dinstein, Dr. Robert Garigue, Richard Guida, Wendy Gully (Archivist, U.S. Navy Submarine Force Museum, Groton, CT.), Ray Gustini, Michael McGuire, Scott Killingsworth, Vince Polley, John Weigelt, Cynthia Trope, Winston Trope, and, for excellent textual editing during the course of the drafting, Dr. Monique Witt.

Any errors or omissions, however, are the responsibility of the authors alone.

We also thank the ABA Cyberspace Committee for its firm support of our efforts; our editors at the American Bar Association, Ms. Suzy Bibko and Ms. Ann Poole, for their assistance and contributions; Ms. Wendy Berry for her assistance on the book's production and distribution; and Mr. Gabriel Guzman for his fine design of this book's cover.

Preface

Hostile environments and adverse consequences are now the norm for organizations whose success depends, in large part, on the management and security of their "information assets."

Directors and executives of such organizations, when asked to consider the protection of their stored business information, often view their organizations as "castles." We believe this fortress metaphor is inadequate to describe the rapidly changing threats to information assets. Instead, Directors should view their organizations as more analogous to modern "submarines." Like corporations, submarines also operate with no view of distant horizons, and the need to monitor and analyze data continuously and assiduously in order to achieve their objectives.

In order to assist Directors in improving their understanding of the hostile environment that confronts organizations with evolving data-related obligations, we have designed a short, pithy exposition of "data governance." It is intended to fit within Directors' and executives' hectic schedules.

This Guide outlines threats, legal "drivers," and questions that Boards should pose to their management regarding the organization's data governance regimes. Directors are not expected to read the endnotes. They are provided for advisers who may wish to delve into fact-specific cases and illustrations provided by the sources.

E. Michael Power
Roland L. Trope

CHAPTER 1

Organizations as Submarines: Why Data Governance Is Imperative

"Human history is more and more a race between education and catastrophe."
—H.G. Wells

Until recently, data governance seldom merited serious discussion by corporate Directors. However, as the emergence of digital technologies and the Internet (and the advent of security risks that can have significant consequences) has drawn attention to information security, it caused corporate Boards to begin to raise these issues. Unfortunately, the primary approach has been one that follows the traditional paradigm of Director and Officer response to emerging risks in areas like corporate governance. Issues are targeted and briefed as risks are identified through litigation. This is an effective strategy where the scope of the risks is basically known. When Directors apply such an approach to information security in the use of information technology and the Internet, however, they are apt to focus too narrowly on known risks and to overlook the need to adopt a broader, comprehensive view of their company's data governance.

For the purposes of this Guide, data governance is defined as the *ongoing management of the risk of unauthorized collection, use, disclosure, transfer, modification, and/or destruction of information through physical, procedural, and technical security mechanisms.*

Data governance is best understood as a combination of the concerns that emerge in connection with: (1) information security (managed by the chief security officer or CSO), (2) record or document retention (often managed by the Chief Financial Officer), and (3) data privacy (managed by the chief privacy officer).[1] Although "information

1

security" now appears routinely on Boardroom agendas, often as a high priority item,[2] the outcomes of such discussions can reflect serious misconceptions and misunderstandings about the nature of the risks to individual companies and their Directors. The responsibilities of various personnel with varying levels of technology expertise, different spheres of responsibility, and the tendency to address these issues "piece-meal" at the Boardroom level further contributes to concerns about the integrity and security of company data governance.[3] What is needed at the Board level is a unified approach. Evolving notions of responsible corporate oversight suggest that Directors need, at a minimum, to comprehend certain basic data governance principles, because they can ill-afford to overlook (or only belatedly appreciate) rapidly evolving risks and exposures.[4]

Those Directors who defer or delegate to specialized personnel their understanding and command of data governance will be at increasing risk of incurring personal liability for failing to fulfill their fiduciary duty of care to ensure that their companies comply with rapidly emerging legal requirements concerning deficiencies in data governance.

When corporate information technology systems suffer damage as a result of vulnerabilities or security breakdowns (referred to hereafter as "incidents"), the costs may range from hundreds of thousands to millions of dollars (including disruption and diagnostic costs as well as ruined or irretrievable data).[5] Such incidents may be caused by unauthorized external access, or carelessness by innocent, well-intentioned personnel, or by insiders exploiting unsuspected vulnerabilities or whose correction had been postponed.

The advent of information technology and the Internet (referred to hereafter as the "Digital Era") has brought about profound changes in risk management, asset protection, and internal reporting. Such changes have occurred because companies have relinquished the relatively static, predictable, and easily controlled conditions of hard copy records for the *dynamic, less predictable, and more difficult to control conditions of digital or electronic records.*[6] Because of these changes, Directors often misunderstand key aspects of data retention and protection. Because in many instances a firm's "assets" are increasingly indistinguishable from its stored information, the integrity of the mode of storage is an integral part of the preservation of its "value." Failure to be aware of this or sufficiently concerned with the integrity of stored information can leave the firm's information assets vulnerable to unauthorized access, misappropriation, modification, damage, or destruction.

Today, a failure to provide appropriate data governance can become a crisis that rapidly undermines the integrity and reputation of the organization. In an environment of increased media attention to privacy and security, the magnitude of "headline" risks and the corresponding loss of the goodwill of customers, partners, regulators, and other stakeholders can have an immediate and profound "bottom line." To the extent information security is seen as a component of critical infrastructure protection in a post 9/11 environment, data governance is also increasingly treated as a critical and integral part of national security.

One tenet of this book is that Directors should adopt data governance standards, both for themselves and their organizations, that exceed what a strict reading of the law today appears to require. For risks that change gradually, when Boards have ample time to respond, there is little need or benefit to push an organization's legal compliance "ahead of the curve." This is especially so when organizations struggle to meet minimum compliance requirements, and we can empathize with Directors who simply want to do what regulators may now require. Most Boards may well "be happy if they felt that they had, for just one brief shining moment, 'caught up' with accepted, mandatory legal requirements."[7]

Where technological risks evolve at an increasingly rapid pace being "caught up" will leave an organization far "behind the curve," reacting belatedly to problems, incurring high costs in damage control, as well as financial and reputational loss. As many companies have learned from late attempts to comply with the Sarbanes Oxley Act, a prudent, early investment to get "ahead of the curve" would have positioned them to reap substantial savings on "best practices" and spared them the need to disclose in an annual report the existence of "material weaknesses in internal controls."

We believe it "penny wise and pound foolish" for a Board to settle for a narrow reading of laws and accept minimal improvements in compliance in areas where the trend among regulators is to adopt ever-more stringent readings of legal requirements. Any perceived "getting ahead of the curve" now simply means "less catch up" later and the avoidance of risk and/or loss in the interim. Board consideration of "data governance" is only just beginning and addressing framework questions now with foresight and a determination that "best practices" should exceed minimal legal requirements will ensure Directors fulfill their personal obligations and corporate duties.

This Guide is intended to help Directors fulfill their obligations by providing them with some practical questions for ensuring the management of inherent risks and emerging foreseeable threats.

In Chapter Two, we review the impending "perfect storm" in the information security environment. We identify seven trends that contribute to its formation, its breadth and intensity, and the severity of its consequences for organizations and their Directors. Chapter Two makes the case that data governance must become a high priority for Directors; and Chapter Three explains why data governance will remain a high priority for Directors for the foreseeable future. In Chapter Three, we review the data governance issues that most warrant Directors' attention. We explain changes in digital asset protection and internal reporting that affect Directors' fiduciary duties and create legal obligations that can expose them to increased risks of personal liability. We highlight the applicable requirements (referred to in this Guide as "drivers"), which we believe create positive obligations and which, if not properly addressed, will be a source of potential liability for Directors. Chapter Three concludes with a summary of key points that are synthesized into a recommended list of priority issues that Directors should explore each time they review internal reports on data governance, specifically in relation to reports that assess and attest to internal controls for financial reporting by their organization and its outsource service providers.

Chapter Four proposes key lines of inquiry that Directors should pursue to assure themselves that data governance receives sufficient attention by supervisory personnel within their organizations. Our premise is that Directors cannot simply adopt the reports prepared by technical personnel or executive officers concerning the enterprise's information security without risking fiduciary liability. Evolving case law and legislation reveal a strong trend toward an increasing Director and Officer obligation to know more and toward increasing categories of "duties to know" that are "non-delegable." This Guide adopts the view that Directors need to ask specific questions and to be less willing to accept on face value initial answers. This will facilitate their moving quickly up the learning curve of what they need to know effectively to supervise their company's data governance.

We emphasize that for an enterprise to succeed at efficient data governance, its Directors must perceive the effort as a continuous process designed not simply to identify imminent risks and to anticipate emerging threats, but also to avert, wherever feasible and practical, unauthorized access to or misuse of the enterprise's information assets. When incidents occur, as they inevitably will in the best-managed enterprises, it is necessary to detect each promptly, to mitigate damages and prevent their spread, and to improve security to reduce the probability of a reoccurrence. Success in this endeavour is a daunting task for management. And shareholders and enforcement agencies will increasingly scrutinize its oversight by Directors as the information technology transformation continues to mature.

We believe it would be useful for Directors to adopt a dynamic image of their company that accurately reflects the need to safeguard valuable but highly mutable information assets. Companies are increasingly less like "castles" with their Boardroom's citadels enjoying a clear view of the far horizons and of approaching attackers. In their use of information technology in daily operations, the companies of the 21st century more often resemble a modern submarine, dependent upon computer systems and continuous scanning to protect against incoming threats. The Boardroom is more like a "conning tower" or bridge. Like a sub captain, a Director must develop the expertise to evaluate the information provided by his company officers in order to clarify the status of the ship.

Changing this paradigm will prepare Directors to treat Company security needs as a high priority and as an on-going concern. It will also permit a well-prepared "damage control" team to identify potential threats quickly, to select the most effective means to contain the damage promptly and to avoid putting the ship and its enterprise in peril. It will help Directors to address the inherent conflict in managing information security—namely that "the compelling desire to achieve [information security] co-exists with an equally compelling desire to enjoy its achievement without further investment of funds or vigilance."[8]

CHAPTER 2

Weather Report:
A Digital Perfect Storm?

"Professor," replied Captain Nemo, "you must not confuse static
and dynamic situations, or you will fall into serious error."
—Jules Verne, *20,000 Leagues Under the Sea*

Directors often do not recognize that their company's protection of
valuable information assets or that company internal controls on financial reporting are premised on an unfounded sense of digital security.
Such oversights occur because Directors are not sufficiently aware of
the impending "perfect storm" in the security environment: develop-
ments have combined to diminish the margins of safety that Directors
believe exist when they review reports on their company's information
security. The elements of this "perfect storm" include seven trends that
we describe in this Chapter.

    1. Unabated Severity and Growing Diversity of Internal Risks. Cor-
porate IT departments devote the majority of their efforts to averting
external threats launched from the Internet, but the majority of successful attacks on corporate computer systems come from *inside* the
target company.[9] The line, however, between persons *inside* and *outside*
of an organization becomes blurred when the organization has outsource service providers or relies on integrated suppliers. Moreover, as
noted in the Financial Times,

> "The central importance of IT systems to business practice has led
> many company boards to regard their business as secure, solely on
> the basis of measures to protect their computer systems. Security
> experts, even those within the IT sector, are now warning that this
> is a wrong approach. . . . 'it's not the technology that is the weakest
> link—it's the people . . . If you have to rely on technology then

you have failed. There is a huge training and education issue that companies tend to ignore when it comes to protecting their systems,' . . . "[10]

Directors must monitor internal risks with even greater vigilance, because, in the Digital Era, internal risks remain the predominant cause of breaches of digital security.[11] A well-managed enterprise will, therefore, be alert to internal risks and vigilantly monitor its information technology systems for signs of unauthorized access from *within* the company and for inappropriate activity launched from within its networks. As an analogous illustration in submarines, the practice in some navies, before casting off, is to pre-test the integrity of the hull (and the diligence of the crew). Hatches are closed and sealed tightly. Pumps evacuate air inside the boat. The higher pressure of the outside air simulates the pressure that will be exerted (with much greater force) by the sea against the submerged boat. The crew then light candles which they slowly and painstakingly pass along all critical seams in the inner hull. They watch the flame. If it wavers, there's an air leak, a hole that water would penetrate with much greater force. Officers watch to check the crew's performance. They do not underestimate or overlook the internal risks of vulnerabilities in the vessel or in the crew.

Digital security requires commensurate care to avert internal breakdowns and breaches. The majority of insider exploits result from insufficient investment in data governance (e.g., poor policy, inadequate processes, and superficial training[12]) or from a violation of trust. Good data governance requires that an organization prepare its personnel to adhere to privacy, retention and security procedures and that it deploy counter-measures to deter and detect breaches of policy or procedure that may result from indifference, carelessness or treachery (by personnel at any level of the organization).

"Unfortunately, few technologies guard against risks from insiders, the source of the highest risks. As reported in the 2002 CSI/FBI survey, 70 percent of successful attacks originate from inside the fortified network boundary.[13] As the GAO explains, "Insiders may not need a great deal of knowledge about computer intrusions because their knowledge of a victim system often allows them to gain unrestricted access to cause damage to the system or to steal system data. The insider threat also includes outsourcing vendors."[14, 15]

2. Decline in Relative Importance of Perimeter Defenses. Companies have historically invested in protective measures based on "fortress-based" security metaphors (e.g., perimeter defenses, defense-in-depth[16]), without understanding "the differences between such metaphors and the realities of securing a system. . . ."[17] The realities are considerably more complex. Over-reliance on perimeter defenses tends to distract attention from insider risks. Moreover, a fortress-derived defense tends to encourage a misplaced reliance on static protections against rapidly changing, dynamic threats. As commentators have observed, the "'build well and maintain indefinitely' nature of a fortress does not suffice."[18]

Moreover, the fortress metaphor is rapidly approaching obsolescence, because company boundaries for IT systems have ceased to delimit a finite space. As these boundaries evolve, security becomes less focused on protecting a company's perimeter and more focused on protecting information assets wherever accessed by the company and third-party service providers.[19] This "blurring of lines" can be seen in:

- *Outsourcing:* Increased outsourcing of services (both onshore and cross-border) has relocated substantial quantities of company IT assets to service vendors; the customer remains accountable for proper handling of that data, particularly where it includes personally identifiable data.
- *Integrated Supply Chains:* Increased integration of supply chains, and the move to "just-in-time" supply relationships results in sensitive or confidential business data moving up stream to suppliers and downstream to distributors and resellers.
- *Mobility of Data:* The proliferation of high density digital media (e.g., CD, DVD, flash memory, keychain drives, etc.) has resulted in copious quantities of company-sensitive data being stored on such media for transport and the wide dispersal of a company's IT assets to multiple off-site locations. Furthermore, as personnel bring such portable storage devices back in across the company's perimeter, such devices are not subject to inspection by the company's security systems.

3. Rapid Evolution of External Threats. Companies currently have far less time to react than they have historically, and should anticipate a digital environment in which pro-active defensive measures are needed to prevent future incidents. The strains of "malicious" code (code designed to sabotage or subvert the integrity and function of information systems, platforms, or architecture) have evolved rapidly as have the skills of their authors. As a result, the elapsed time between a vendor's disclosure of a critical vulnerability in its software and the commencement of cyber-attacks that exploit such vulnerability has been compressed from months to days. We anticipate a near-term scenario of so-called "zero-day" attacks (based on vulnerabilities that hackers discover before vendors do, and that result in cyber-attacks for which vendors have not yet released or developed a remedial patch).[20]

We also anticipate that the most severe, foreseeable threats are state-sponsored cyber-attacks that aim to conduct corporate espionage or to disrupt or destroy substantial segments of the nation's information system infrastructure. As one observer explains:

> "[T]he Internet and the World Wide Web are ideally suited for asymmetrical warfare and corporate espionage. They can be used by states and nonstate actors to *anonymously* pry into a state's public, sensitive, and classified computers; . . . to manipulate data; to deceive decision makers; . . . and to even cause physical destruction from remote locations abroad. . . . [C]ommercial businesses and computer-dependent commercial infrastructures are likely the most lucrative targets during armed conflict between states in CyberSpace where the opportunity exists to bring a stock exchange, and perhaps the economy of an entire state, to its knees. . . . A hostile state could correctly assume that a state's businesses and critical infrastructures are its soft underbelly that is easier to hit than hardened military targets. . . . Suffice it to say that the disruption, manipulation, and destruction of data via the Internet promises to be sufficiently disruptive that military applications of CyberSpace are sure to be developed and utilized in the near future."[21]

Unless an enterprise has in place a system for the early detection of such attacks, and has prepared and rehearsed means to quarantine and protect its information technology systems, it will suffer potentially irreparable damage. The evolution of external threats should prompt Directors and Officers to ensure their enterprise is prepared for such worst-case scenarios, since their occurrence is increasingly probable.

4. Continued Production and Use of Vulnerable Software. At the beginning of the Digital Era, Company personnel were primarily focused on the instability and unreliability of computer system software. While these interrupted or delayed transactions, they did not threaten the on-going economic viability of the business enterprise. Such failures prompted complaints about deficiencies or flaws that made the performance of information technology systems unreliable and unpredictable. Complaints about "buggy software" drew attention away from deficiencies and flaws in security because the latter weaknesses were not initially as costly or troublesome. Systems that crashed or performed erratically became a higher priority in the Boardrooms than systems that could be sabotaged with "malwares," because sabotage was not yet a common occurrence.

The times, however, have changed. And because software developers initially did not design software that would be secure from unauthorized access, they gave little attention to discovering and removing vulnerabilities. Recent efforts to teach (or retrain) programmers to write (and to make it a priority to write) secure code are viewed by some observers as "failing miserably."[22] Vendors continue to make post-delivery discoveries of critical vulnerabilities and to release remedial patches, often encouraging customers to download the patches "automatically" and to install them without testing. However, the automated updates or patches fail to address two fundamental problems: that unimproved programming creates vulnerability-ridden software[23] and that issuance of remediation patches cannot keep pace with the emerging threats.[24] Installation of insecure code on a firm's computer renders its IT systems insecure regardless of any or all subsequently added safeguards.

5. *Legal Trends Imposing Liability.* As described below, federal and state statutes continue to emerge that impose such burdensome compliance costs and complex compliance requirements that companies often achieve only superficial compliance.[25] Moreover, recent judicial decisions have increasingly held responsible personnel as well as supervisory personnel (i.e., Directors and Officers) liable for failure to fulfill their fiduciary and other obligations to remediate deficient security. As one commentator recently observed,

"Three legal trends are rapidly shaping the information security landscape for most companies. They are:

- an increasing recognition that providing information security is a corporate legal obligation;
- the emergence of a legal standard against which compliance with that obligation will be measured; and
- a new emphasis on a duty to disclose breaches of information security.

While the law is still developing, and is often applied only in selective areas, these three trends are posing significant new challenges for most businesses."[26]

Moreover, the federal enforcement agencies appear to be increasingly focusing on corporate implementation of regulations and rules concerning the implementation of an enterprise-wide legal compliance program. For example, in February 2004, the Securities and Exchange Commission ("SEC") adopted rules requiring registered investment advisers and funds to adopt and implement:

> "written policies and procedures reasonably designed to prevent violation of the federal securities laws, review those policies and procedures annually for their adequacy and the effectiveness of their implementation, and designate a chief compliance officer to be responsible for administering the policies and procedures. In the case of an investment company, the chief compliance officer will report directly to the fund board."[27]

SEC staff reportedly began "telephoning investment companies to gauge their compliance with the SEC's new chief compliance officer ("CCO") rules" and asked the CCO's a range of questions such as whether the CCO believes "he or she has sufficient resources to implement the new compliance program" and whether "the anticipated nature of the working relationship between the fund's Board of Directors and the CCO had been considered."[28]

Federal regulatory agencies have even issued pre-emptive directives that bar an enterprise from embarking on major transactions until the enterprise corrects deficiencies in its internal controls, which certainly should include measures to safeguard the security of the enterprise's financial information. For example, in March 2005, when the Federal Reserve Board approved Citigroup's application to acquire a Texas bank, the Fed's order noted "deficiencies" in legal compliance and internal controls, and reportedly instructed Citigroup "to delay plans for big takeovers until it tightens internal controls and addresses regulatory problems at home and abroad."[29]

6. Investor Scrutiny of Company Information Security. However reasonable in scope and implementation, if digital protections nonetheless fail and a security breach causes immediate, long-term disruption of business operations (longer than 48 hours[30]), the investing public can be expected to judge harshly a company that allowed its business continuity to be jeopardized.[31] For public companies, Directors must respond to the information security pressures of the market that may result, for example, from depressed stock prices triggered by security breaches.

7. Reliance on the Wrong Assumption. Officers and Directors, who seek to comply with legal requirements to assess and report on the status of their internal controls for the company's financial reporting, seldom recognize that they are assuming the existence of an illusion—digital security. The first obstacle to address is the common misconception *that company information technology ("IT") systems are "presumptively" safe.* This presumption of safety reflects misplaced trust in inadequately understood and insufficiently examined IT systems and internal controls. *The presumption should instead be that IT systems are at high risk of compromise from internal and external sources. And systems should be deemed insecure until proven otherwise.*[32] Enhanced dependency on electronically stored records and other information assets has also enhanced vulnerability to breaches in security. Such breaches permit unauthorized access to confidential, sensitive, and valuable information, and can cause it to be misappropriated, modified without the company's knowledge, damaged, or destroyed.

Whether the cascade of security breaches in the first six months of 2005 reflect an increased frequency of such incidents[33] or a perceived need by organizations to notify customers and clients of such incidents or both, the number of records compromised in each instance is substantial and the problems—reputational, financial, and legal—for the companies that have suffered the incidents should prompt Directors to recalibrate the nature, magnitude, and precautions necessary to avert such risks.

From those seven trends, we think it reasonable to infer that digital protection and security of an enterprise's information assets should be a high priority for Directors and Officers, and should remain so for the foreseeable future. Moreover, as we demonstrate in the next Chapter, the emerging legal "drivers" impose duties on Directors to ensure that management devotes sufficient attention and resources to avert threats and risks that the enterprise anticipates could result in unauthorized access or damage to, or misuse of, information assets (whether such assets are proprietary data, personally identifiable information, or records the enterprise has an obligation to retain and preserve).

CHAPTER 3

The Present and Emerging Seascape: Legal Obligations and Risks

This Chapter will illustrate the various security obligations or "drivers" that have emerged that make information and organizational security a topic that should be routinely and systematically addressed by Boards.

A. Fulfillment of Fiduciary Duty of Care

Evolving case law suggests that persons entrusted with fiduciary duties, such as corporate Directors, will find their duty of care extended by courts to include a company's information security systems. And they will find themselves in breach of such duties if the protective measures do not ensure a high degree of security for such assets and internal controls. As a result, Directors may increasingly find their supervisory responsibility "will extend from safeguarding corporate financial data accuracy to safeguarding the integrity of all stored data."[34]

Traditionally, persons entrusted with funds had a fiduciary duty of care to safeguard and ensure the security of such assets. Fulfillment of such fiduciary duties—for *protection, security,* and *accounting*—can be illustrated by reference to a "lockbox." If persons entrusted with funds did not take reasonable precautions to store the assets in a secure location with appropriate safeguards—such as a bank lockbox—they would have difficulty demonstrating that they had fulfilled their fiduciary obligation to *protect and safeguard* the asset. Moreover, they would be at heightened risk of failing to provide an accurate accounting of the asset or would jeopardize the "res" or the subject matter of the trust.

The trustee or fiduciary could assume that the asset would not change while stored in the box. Even if the asset were valuable information in hard copy (such as a will or deed or trade secret), the same principle applied: paper records would in all likelihood remain intact. They retained their integrity, confidentiality, availability, and thus their accountability.[35] If someone broke into the lockbox, he might remove the documents, but unauthorized entry would not thereby modify the asset.

By contrast, when valuable or sensitive information is stored on digital media, there is a fundamental change in its "permanence" and the "immutability" of its content that extends the scope of Directors' fiduciary duty of care. The mode of storing the information asset and the asset itself are no longer "separable." *Putting information assets into a digital lockbox (such as a computer's hard drive) makes those assets virtually an inseparable part of that storage unit.*[36] If a digital storage unit is altered by a virus,[37] worm,[38] Trojan, or other malicious code, the information stored on it is often tampered with and altered. If a hacker (from outside) or an employee or officer (from inside) gains unauthorized access into a computer network, he can "affect" its contents not only by removing or destroying the physical "res," but also by copying or modifying the information asset. Since the asset and digital medium on which it is stored have become inseparable, the *protection, security,* and *accounting* of the asset merges with the protection, security, and accounting of the method of storage. The data asset is itself a box, and that changes fundamentally the way Directors look at it.

The inseparability of the information asset from the digital media is further demonstrated by the unique nature of digital recording. Depending upon the software that the organization uses, creating or storing a document in electronic digital media also may create information about that document (such as the identity of its author, dates of creation and modification, and changes made to the text during various revisions) that is not visible if the document is printed in hard copy, but can be viewed in the digital media (by looking at what is called the document's "metadata").

Attacks on the digital lockbox are attacks on the information assets (the digitized data). They are also attacks on the internal controls on which the accounting and public reporting of those assets depend. The scope of Directors' fiduciary duty of care extends as a result from the asset to the means of storing it (and to the internal controls).[39] Consequently, the digitizing of information assets and storage of such assets on computers connected to the Internet has transformed the calculus of risks for which fiduciaries have a duty of care. *Directors can fulfill their fiduciary duty of care for digital assets only by also safeguarding the digital system.*

Whereas a paper document stored in a locked box is stable, the same information asset when stored in digital media, without appropriate safeguards[40] becomes dynamic, changeable by operations of the computer and by operations of unauthorized personnel.[41] If an entity has chosen to store sensitive data, such as financial records, on a computer, recent cases suggest that the persons entrusted with the care of such funds have a fiduciary duty for the digital protection and security required to keep such data accurate, confidential, and accessible (seemingly incompatible goals).[42]

A recent decision by the U.S. Court of Appeals for the District of Columbia, in *Corbell v. Norton*, amply illustrates the extended scope of that duty. The case involved the federal government's trusteeship for revenues obtained from native American tribal lands (e.g., from granting oil and gas easements), which the government holds in trust for Indian beneficiaries in Individual Indian Money ("IIM") accounts and for which the government has a fiduciary obligation to provide an accounting. Unfortunately, the government neglected its obligations, allowed the Treasury Department to destroy paper records containing IIM trust data ("IIMTD"), belatedly stored IIMTD on Department of Interior ("Interior") computers, and failed to take measures to avoid substantial deficiencies in digital protection and security that left the IIMTD accessible to unauthorized persons seeking access from the Internet.

Indian beneficiaries filed a class-action suit to require the federal government to fulfill its fiduciary obligations. The government denied that it owed the IIMTD a fiduciary duty of care and that, even if it did, that such duty did not extend to providing digital protection and security for such information assets. The District Court decided in favour of the Indian beneficiaries with respect to the government's fiduciary duty of care, a decision affirmed by the Court of Appeals.

When the District Court learned from a Special Master's investigation that Interior's computers contained numerous critical deficiencies in digital security, the District Court issued an injunction ordering Interior to disconnect from the Internet all computers within its control that contained or provided access to IIMTD. The Special Master gradually permitted Interior to reconnect almost all of its computers, but ordered the testing of the reconnected systems and found them deficient in digital security with respect to threats from the Internet. The District

Court then issued a new order to Interior to disconnect its computers from the Internet.

As a result of procedural errors by the District Court (such as failing to hold a hearing before issuing its latest injunction), the Court of Appeals reversed and remanded on December 3, 2004. Significantly, however, the Court of Appeals held that the District Court's "jurisdiction properly extends to security of Interior's information technology systems ... housing or accessing [trust data], because [Interior] ... as a fiduciary, is required to maintain and preserve" such data. The Court further noted that Interior "has current and prospective trust management duties that necessitate maintaining secure IT systems in order to render accurate accountings now and in the future," implying a *fiduciary duty for digital security*. The Court of Appeals thereby suggested its willingness to hold senior officials responsible for highly technical knowledge and to hold them liable for breach of their fiduciary duty of care if they relied on a deficient digital protection system to safeguard "*information assets whose digital integrity is essential to safeguarding financial assets.*"[43]

B. Compliance with *Sarbanes-Oxley Act of 2002*

Congressional enactment of the Foreign Corrupt Practices Act of 1977 amended the Securities Exchange Act of 1934 to require that public companies create and maintain internal accounting controls. As one commentator explains: "These controls must, among other things, provide 'reasonable assurance' that transactions occur only in accordance with management's authorization ..."[44] The *Sarbanes-Oxley Act* of 2002 ("SOX")[45] raised the standards for management's attention to internal controls.

SOX affects a broad spectrum of companies whose stock is publicly traded on a U.S. exchange. Of particular significance to data governance is the emphasis that SOX places on the creation, evaluation, assessment, and correction of the registrant's "internal controls" for financial reporting. The emphasis is reflected in two sections: 302 and 404.

Section 302 requires the officers who sign the company's annual report to *certify* that they have reviewed it to ensure (i) that it does not contain any untrue statement of a material fact, or omit to state a material fact necessary to make the statement not be misleading and (ii) that the financial statements and other financial information fairly present the financial condition and results of operations of the registrant.

Section 302 also makes the signing officers responsible for (i) establishing and maintaining the registrant's "internal controls"; (ii) designing those controls to ensure that the registrant's officers receive material information relating to the registrant and its consolidated subsidiaries; (iii) evaluating the registrant's "internal controls" within the previous 90 days; and (iv) reporting the results of their evaluation, which must include:

- a list of all "material weaknesses" found in the "internal controls;"
- any fraud found in such controls;
- any significant changes that could negatively affect such controls; and
- the corrections taken with respect to any material weakness or significant deficiencies in those controls.

Section 404 requires the registrant to include in its annual report an *internal control report,* which must: (i) state management's responsibility to establish and maintain internal controls for the registrant's financial reporting; and (ii) contain an assessment as of the end of the registrant's most recent fiscal year of the effectiveness of the internal control structure and procedures for financial reporting.[46] As explained in the SEC's Final Rule on "Management's Reports on Internal Control Over Financial Reporting and Certification of Disclosure in Exchange Act Periodic Reports" (effective August 14, 2003) ("Final Rule"):

"The assessment of a company's internal control over financial reporting must be based on procedures sufficient both to evaluate its design and to test its operating effectiveness. . . . [and] must be supported by evidential matter, including documentation, regarding both the design of internal controls and the testing processes."[47]

In addition, the Final Rule required not only an annual assessment of internal controls, but disclosure, in quarterly reports, of any change that materially affects internal controls:

"[A] company must disclose any change in its internal control over financial reporting that occurred during the fiscal quarter covered by the quarterly report, or the last fiscal quarter in the case of an annual report, that has materially affected, or is reasonably likely to materially affect, the company's internal control over financial reporting."[48]

Of particular concern to registrants, is the Final Rule's requirement that management identify and disclose "material weaknesses" in internal controls, and that existence of such weaknesses *precludes* an assessment that internal controls are effective:

"This discussion [management's assessment] must include disclosure of any material weakness in the registrant's internal control over financial reporting identified by management. Management is not permitted to conclude that the registrant's internal control over financial reporting is effective if there are one or more material weaknesses in the registrant's internal control over financial reporting."[49]

Although a number of companies reported "material weaknesses" in the first year of Section 404's implementation, the SEC's Corporate Division Staff has made clear that merely mentioning that such "weaknesses" exist is *not* sufficient:

"The staff believes that, as a result, companies should consider including in their disclosures:

• the nature of any material weakness,
• its impact on financial reporting and the control environment, and
• management's current plans, if any, for remediating the weakness."[50]

Some security professional groups contend that when Section 404 is read together with guidance published by the SOX-mandated Public Company Accounting Oversight Board ("PCAOB"), such "materials pinpoint obligations" for registrants "to secure those information technology systems essential for the integrity of financial reporting."[51] Such interpretations attempt to read requirements into SOX that simply do not exist in its text. But all registrants undoubtedly have internal controls whose implementation is achieved through information technology systems and whose integrity therefore depends on effective digital protections and security. As the PCAOB observes in Audit Standard No. 2, "[t]he nature and characteristics of a company's use of information technology in its information system affect the company's control over financial reporting."[52]

The causal relationship between the status of a registrant's information security and the quality of its internal controls over financial reporting received helpful clarification in May 2005, when the SEC's Division of Corporation Finance Staff issued a "Statement on Management's Report on Internal Control Over Financial Reporting."[53]

"[T]he staff expects management to document and test relevant general IT [information technology] controls in addition to appropriate application-level controls that are designed to ensure that financial information generated from a company's application systems can reasonably be relied upon. . . . However, the staff does not believe it necessary for purposes of Section 404 for management to assess all general IT controls, and especially not those . . . not relevant to financial reporting."[54]

Since implementation of new IT systems and upgrades may, and often do, introduce new vulnerabilities and risks, the SEC staff addressed management's need to assess such changes without delay:

"[C]ompanies are required to prepare reliable financial statements following the implementation of the new information systems. . . . Some of the feedback requested that management be allowed to exclude new IT systems and upgrades implemented in the later part of a fiscal year from the scope of management's assessment for that year . . . However, with respect to system changes, management can plan, design, and perform preliminary assessments of internal controls in advance of system implementations or upgrades. . . . As a result, the staff does not believe it is appropriate to provide an exclusion by management of new IT systems and upgrades from the scope of its assessment of internal control over financial reporting."[55]

In light of these very real concerns, Directors must verify whether their company has implemented information technology system controls, whether such controls contain significant deficiencies and, if so, whether such deficiencies affect other controls to the extent that financial reporting is potentially inaccurate or misleading. The need for such scrutiny is reinforced by the fact that the SEC rule[56] on SOX Section 404 management reports defines "internal control over financial reporting" as policies and procedures that "provide reasonable assurance regarding *prevention or timely detection of unauthorized acquisition, use or disposition of the registrant's assets* that could have a material effect on the financial statements."[57] Directors should also be aware of the regulatory staff caution that: "where management has outsourced . . . functions to third party service provider(s), management maintains a responsibility to assess the controls over the outsourced operations."[58]

C. Compliance with the *Health Insurance Portability and Accountability Act* (HIPAA)

Although designed primarily for the health care industry, HIPAA's information security requirements deserve attention by most companies and their Directors, because some of the standards it contains may be borrowed by other statutory regimes and they provide one measure of best practices for information security.

HIPAA[59] seeks to "provide insurance portability, fraud enforcement, and administrative simplification"[60] for an industry that Congress recognized to be late and deficient in ensuring protections, privacy, security, and availability of the "protected health information" ("PHI") entrusted to it.[61] The Department of Health and Human Services has published two rules for achieving those objectives: the Privacy Rule, which regulates the disclosure of PHI and sets standards for safeguarding it;[62] and the Security Rule,[63] which sets standards for the confidentiality, integrity, and availability of *electronic* protected health information ("EPHI").[64] Covered entities (except for small health plans)—defined to be health plans, health care clearinghouses, and certain health care providers—had to comply with the final rule by April 20, 2005. Small health plans (with annual receipts of five million or less) have until April 20, 2006 to comply.

The Security Rule sets out 18 standards for safeguarding EPHI. A covered entity must comply with all of those standards.[65] The Security Rule also sets out 42 implementation specifications for those standards. These specifications are distinguished by whether or not their implementation is mandatory under the Security Rule. Implementation of 20 of the specifications is designated "required." A covered entity must implement and comply with each such implementation specification. Implementation of 22 other specifications is designated "addressable." With respect to "addressable" specifications, a covered entity must determine whether the specification is a "reasonable and appropriate safeguard in its environment;" if so it must comply with it. If a covered entity determines the specification is not "reasonable and appropriate," the entity must document its reasons, implement an equivalent alternative measure, and document how that measure ensures compliance with the applicable standard.[66]

To ensure compliance with the Security Rule, the Department of Health and Human Services anticipates that each covered entity "will need to assess existing security, identify areas of risk, and implement additional measures in order to come into compliance with the [Security Rule] standards" and thus "will need to conduct some level of gap analysis to assess [its] current procedures against the [Security Rule] standards."[67] Such assessments will, of course, need to identify gaps between current procedures and each of the standards that the covered entity is "required" to implement, as well as each of the standards whose implementation is "addressable" and that the covered entity determines to be a "reasonable and appropriate safeguard in its environment." As one commentator observes, covered entities have "the flexibility to make their own choices based on their risks, but there must be genuine and documented business reasons behind these decisions."[68]

In doing so they will need to (i) assess potential risks and vulnerabilities to health information in their possession in electronic form; (ii) develop, implement, and maintain appropriate security measures to protect that information; and (iii) document and keep such measures current. Moreover, covered entities must maintain a written record of any action, activity, or assessment they conduct required by the Security Rule, and retain such documentation (for the longer of six years from the date the document was created or from when it last was in effect).[69] Also, the covered entity must review "documentation periodically" and update it "as needed, in response to environmental or operational changes affecting the security of the electronic protected health information."[70]

Directors of covered entities need to be aware that certain on-going record keeping must be maintained concerning any disclosure of protected health information. If such records are not maintained and kept accessible, the covered entity could not be in a position to comply with the requirement that an individual has "a right to receive an accounting of disclosures made by a covered entity in the **six years** prior to the date on which the accounting is requested,"[71] which must include substantial detail of each such disclosure.[72] Care must also be taken to avoid reporting to the requesting individual any disclosure that the HIPAA regulations do not entitle the individual to receive[73] and to comply with the complex requirements concerning "prompt notice" to individuals when certain disclosures are made of their protected health information.[74] Directors, therefore, need to ensure that senior management has established a comprehensive system for determining when the conditions have been met that permit such disclosures, what can be disclosed in that event, whether such disclosure triggers a requirement to notify the individual and, in any event, keep an ongoing accurate record of each such disclosure.[75]

In pursuit of its prescribed standards, the Security Rule sets a very high standard for awareness of emerging threats, particularly those that receive widespread attention or that personnel inside the company have reported up-the-chain as warranting attention. Directors seeking to oversee internal controls and information technology general controls must therefore ensure that reports of "reasonably anticipated threats or hazards" are not filtered out as they percolate up the chain of command. Under HIPAA, such treatment of reports can foreseeably cause a non-compliance with the standard to protect against "reasonably anticipated threats." If a submarine's crew filtered out information in a similar manner, the resulting tactical picture would omit until the last possible moment any display of a serious threat, at which point the "pinging" of an enemy's active sonar would bypass the chain of command and belatedly alert everyone on board to the imminent peril.[76]

D. Compliance with the *Gramm-Leach-Bliley Financial Services Modernization Act of 1999 ("GLBA")*

Title V of GLBA establishes privacy obligations for financial institutions in the United States, and specifically that each financial institution "has an affirmative and continuing obligation to respect the privacy of its customers and to protect the security and confidentiality of those customers' nonpublic personal information."[77] GLBA requires the Federal Trade Commission ("FTC") (among other federal and state agencies) to establish appropriate standards relating to administrative, technical, and physical safeguards:

"(1) to insure the security and confidentiality of customer records and information; (2) to against any anticipated threats or hazards to the security or integrity of such records; and (3) to protect against unauthorized access to or use of such records or information which could result in substantial harm or inconvenience to any customer."[78]

The FTC issued the final "Safeguards Rule," in May 2002, to implement the safeguard provisions of the GLBA.[79]

The Safeguards Rule applies to businesses, regardless of size, provided they are "significantly engaged" in providing financial products or services to consumers[80] and requires such financial institutions to develop and implement a written information security program—the sophistication of which is governed by the institution's size and complexity, the nature and scope of its activities, and the sensitivity of the customer information. To be compliant, such programs must contain certain elements, including:

(a)   an identification and assessment of risks to customer information "in each relevant area of the company's operation;"

(b)   an evaluation of the effectiveness of the company's current safeguards for controlling those identified risks;

(c)   a safeguards program, which addresses at a minimum three areas that the FTC believes are particularly relevant to information security:
i. employee management and training,
ii. information systems (e.g., data storage, transmission, and disposal), and
iii. managing system failures.[81]

The safeguards program is not to be a static, one-time effort, but instead the company must regularly monitor and test it.[82]

The FTC adopts the view that features of information security, often perceived by companies and their management to be *constants*, are actually *variables* and should be monitored for changes to which the companies should respond accordingly. For example, the FTC views each of the following as an ever-changing or potentially changing variable.

Security Breaches

The FTC assumes that security breaches will occur and vary considerably, and thus security programs should be designed and implemented accordingly. The FTC insisted in the Safeguards Rule that each financial institution assure itself that its "current and potential service providers maintain sufficient procedures to detect and respond to security breaches" and that each financial institution "maintain reasonable procedures to discover and respond to widely-known security failures by its current and potential service providers."[83]

Material Changes

The Safeguards Rule requires each institution to "evaluate and adjust its information security program 'in light of the results of the testing and monitoring required [by the Rule] . . . any material changes to operations or business arrangements [e.g., mergers, acquisitions, alliances, joint ventures, and outsourcings]; or any other circumstances that you know or have reason to know may have a material impact on [the institution's] information security program."[84]

The four principal agencies that regulate financial institutions covered by GLBA[85] issued on January 17, 2001 their *Interagency Guidance Establishing Standards for Safeguarding Customer Information*,[86] and on August 12, 2003, the same agencies issued for public comment their *Interagency Guidance on Response Programs for Unauthorized Access to Customer Information and Customer Notice*. In March 2005, the four agencies jointly issued *Interagency Guidance on Response Programs for Unauthorized Access to Customer Information and Customer Notice* which constitutes "final guidance" ("Guidance")[87] and interprets Section 501(b) of the GLBA and the four agencies' security guidelines[88] ("Security Guidelines") concerning customer information security standards. The *Guidance* provides that:

- Financial institutions should implement an incident response program to address security breaches involving customer information.
- An institution's incident response program should include *at a minimum* procedures for:

  "(a) assessing the nature and scope of an incident, and identifying what customer information systems and types of customer information have been accessed or misused;

  (b) notifying its primary Federal regulator as soon as possible when the institution becomes aware of an incident involving unauthorized access to or use of sensitive customer information . . . ;

(c) immediately notifying law enforcement in situations involving federal criminal violations requiring immediate attention;

(d) taking appropriate steps to contain and control the incident to prevent further unauthorized access to or use of customer information, such as by monitoring, freezing, or closing affected accounts, while preserving records and other evidence; and

(e) notifying customers when warranted."[89]

The Guidelines set a standard for when a financial institution becomes obligated to give such notice to its customers as part of its incident response compliance.[90] The trigger for notice is access to "sensitive customer information"[91] where the financial institution determines that misuse of such information "has occurred or is reasonably possible."[92] As the final Guidelines observe:

"Timely notification of customers is important to manage an institution's reputation risk. Effective notice also may reduce an institution's legal risk, assist in maintaining good customer relations, and enable the institution's customers to take steps to protect themselves against the consequences of identity theft."[93]

Although the final Guidelines do not constitute binding rules for organizations other than financial institutions, the final Guidelines reflect careful thinking on information security, and therefore deserve to be viewed as providing strong recommendations for companies that seek to create good data governance programs and avoid being held liable for deficiencies in information security.

The FTC took its first enforcement actions under the GLBA in November 2004, charging two mortgage companies, Nationwide Mortgage Group, Inc. ("Nationwide") and Sunbelt Lending Services, Inc. ("Sunbelt") with violating the Safeguards Rule by "not having reasonable protections for customers' sensitive personal and financial information." In particular, both companies failed to assess the risks to sensitive customer information and to implement safeguards accordingly. In addition, Nationwide failed to train its employees on information security, or to oversee its loan officers' handling of customer information *or to monitor its computer network for vulnerabilities.* Nationwide also failed, as required, to provide privacy notices to its customers, and Sunbelt failed to provide such notices to its online customers. Sunbelt entered into a settlement with the FTC. The FTC has issued an administrative complaint against Nationwide.[94]

As with the standards we highlighted in our brief review of HIPAA, the GLBA Safeguards Rule should be taken account of by Directors not only of financial institutions but of any company seeking to establish an information security program that will be effective against security threats *and that can be defended if scrutinized by enforcement agencies, potential plaintiffs, courts, or juries.* Borrowing standards from such legislative regimes is eminently defensible, and if documented as an attempt to attain a best practice standard (in the absence of any national standard), the resulting program should help protect a company (and its Directors and Officers) against allegations that certain protective measures, in hindsight, would have averted a security breach and its resulting damage.[95]

E. Compliance with U.S. Federal Sentencing Guidelines

On November 1, 2004, amendments to the United States Sentencing Guidelines took effect, which raised the standards for an organization's "effective legal compliance program" and increased the responsibility of Boards of Directors and executives for the oversight and management of such programs. Although the Sentencing Guidelines have recently been held by the U.S. Supreme Court to be no longer mandatory for determination of a sentence, the Supreme Court also made clear that sentencing judges must "consider" the Sentencing Guidelines when determining a sentence.[96] In view of the continuing relevance of the Sentencing Guidelines, Directors and executives should be aware that for their organization's legal compliance program to qualify as "effective" under the Sentencing Guidelines, they must take an active leadership role for the content and operation of their organization's compliance and ethics programs. The Sentencing Guidelines are intended to strengthen the existing criteria an organization must follow to establish and maintain an effective program to prevent and detect criminal conduct for purposes of distancing the company from "aggravating" factors (and qualifying the company for the benefits of "mitigating" factors) in the event of enforcement action.[97]

In view of the emerging legal requirements for information security, it is important for Directors to ensure that their company has an "effective legal compliance program" in order to reduce the chances of enforcement action and to diminish the potential penalties that might be imposed. An effective compliance and ethics program should not only diminish and detect criminal conduct, but should also facilitate compliance with all applicable laws.[98]

F. Compliance with State Laws

California Identity Theft Prevention Law

California statute SB 1386,[99] in force as of July 1, 2003 and amending the California Civil Code, was enacted in response to the increasing concerns about identity theft, principally as a result of the compromise of personal information collected and held by organizations. The law requires a state agency, or a person or business that conducts business in California and that owns or licenses computerized data that includes "personal information" to disclose in specified ways any "breach of the security" of the data to any resident of California whose unencrypted "personal information" was, or is reasonably believed to have been, acquired by an unauthorized person.[100] "Breach of the security of the system" is defined to mean "unauthorized acquisition of computerized data that compromises the security, confidentiality, or integrity of personal information maintained by the agency."[101]

These amendments have arguably an extra-territorial application to the extent that they apply to organizations holding data on California residents, who may find themselves subject to Californian courts asserting jurisdiction—especially given potential significant penalties that can be inflicted by class-action lawsuits, including penalties for negligence in exercising an adequate standard of care with respect to information security. The California Office of Privacy Protection has published recommended practices for providing notice in cases of security breach involving personal information.[102]

The impact that SB 1386's reporting requirements can have on an organization's efforts to contain and control the consequences of a security breach was well illustrated when ChoicePoint (one of the largest sellers of private consumer data) learned that an apparent identity theft ring had gained unauthorized access to its databases. California police subsequently concluded that from ChoicePoint's "19 billion data files" vulnerable data had been "downloaded on millions of people, and used to run up millions of fraudulent credit card charges."[103] The breach reportedly occurred in October 2004. In mid-February 2005, under compulsion of SB 1386, ChoicePoint sent e-mail notifications to all customers residing in California, alerting them to the breach and risks it posed to the security of their personal records and finances.[104] The first of several class action suits based on the incident was filed less than a week later against ChoicePoint.[105] Attorneys general in 18 other states learned of the notice and informed ChoicePoint that they also required notice to citizens in their states, with the result that ChoicePoint eventually decided to notify all customers.[106] By mid-March 2005, ChoicePoint's chairman and CEO was testifying before a subcommittee of the House of Representatives where he offered a public apology on behalf of ChoicePoint and himself for "fraudulent activity ChoicePoint failed to prevent."[107] As *The Wall Street Journal* noted, "The security lapse at ChoicePoint . . . would likely still be under wraps if not for a California law [SB 1386] requiring consumers to be notified if their private data is stolen."[108]

As of May 2005, Arkansas,[109] Georgia,[110] Montana,[111] North Dakota,[112] and Washington[113] have enacted similar notification laws.

Pennsylvania's Deceptive Privacy Law

Section 4107 of Title 18 of the Pennsylvania Consolidated Statutes was amended on November 20, 2004 to make it a misdemeanor[114] if any person "intentionally, knowingly or recklessly" in the course of business "knowingly makes a false or misleading statement in a privacy policy, published on the Internet or otherwise distributed or published, regarding the use of personal information submitted by members of the public."

However, the statute expressly does not apply to a financial institution (as defined by the GLBA), a covered entity (as defined by HIPAA) or the licensee of such institution or entity. All other companies are subject to the new statute. For Directors, compliance will probably require their company to engage in a two-stage diligence process: to check privacy policies against existing company practices prior to publication; and to make similar checks routinely to verify whether practices have deviated from such policies (and if so to remediate them promptly).

G. Complying with Risk Management Requirements Under Basel II

Under the auspices of the Bank of International Settlements, the Basel Committee on Banking Supervision[115] finalized a new international capital standard known as Basel II in June 2004.[116] Basel II represents a major revision of the international standard on bank capital adequacy that was introduced in 1988, and is intended to "modernize" the capital measurement framework and enhance financial stability by promoting better risk management. "Basel II . . . mark[s] a significant shift in international capital rules by allowing banks to match their capital more closely with their risk profile. . . . Regulators are still feeling their way over the sort of internal models that banks should be able to develop to monitor their credit risk. They will have to plot the likelihood of loan default and the possible size of loss from defaults. If banks' computer models are approved by regulators, they will be able to hold lower levels of capital than at present."[117] As explained recently by Governor Mark W. Olson of the Federal Reserve Board:

> "Basel II represents an improved and broadly comparable way to look at risk taking across organizations and over time. . . . The framework is structured to be much more risk-sensitive than its predecessor; . . . Basel II is designed to address the concern that Basel I regulatory capital ratios are no longer good indicators of risk for our largest institutions. . . . Basel I presents an opportunity for banks to retain balance-sheet positions that are of higher risk than their regulatory capital charge and to shed those of lower risk. Using this type of capital arbitrage, banks can game the system in such a way that the resultant Basel I ratio does not have substantial meaning for the public, bank management, or the supervisor. Basel II is intended to close this gap by more directly linking riskiness of assets to their corresponding regulatory capital charge and to reduce, if not eliminate, the incentives to engage in capital arbitrage.
>
> Basel II also creates a link between regulatory capital and risk management, especially under the advanced approaches, which are the only ones expected to be applied in the United States. Under these approaches, banks will be required to adopt more formal, quantitative risk-measurement and management procedures and processes. And, to implement this framework, both bank manage-

ment and supervisors will need to focus on the integrity and sound-
ness of these procedures and processes, including comprehensive
assessments of capital adequacy in relation to the bank's overall risk
taking."[118]

Under Basel II, risk management includes "operational risk," which
is defined as the "risk of loss resulting from inadequate or failed internal
processes, people and systems or from external events. This definition
includes legal risk,[119] but excludes strategic and reputational risk."[120]
Basel II recognizes three methods for calculating operational risk capital
charges. The three methods reflect a continuum of increasing sophistication and risk sensitivity: (i) the Basic Indicator Approach; (ii) the
Standardised Approach; and (iii) Advanced Measurement Approach.[121]
In order for a bank to qualify to use either of the two more sophisticated
approaches, it must satisfy its supervisor that, *at a minimum*:

- "its board of directors and senior management, as appropriate, are
  actively involved in the oversight of the **operational risk** management framework;
- it has an operational risk management system that is conceptually
  sound and is implemented with integrity; and
- it has sufficient resources in the use of the approach in the major
  business lines as well as the control and audit areas."[122]

To make use of the more sophisticated approaches, a bank must,
among other things, make regular reports of operational risk exposures
and loss experience to business unit management, senior management
and its Board of Directors. Also, each such bank must "must have a
routine in place for ensuring compliance with a documented set of
internal policies, controls and procedures concerning the operational
risk management system, which must include policies for the treatment
of non-compliance issues."[123]

Generally, until the implementation of Basel II (which will become
compulsory for most EU banks from 2007[124]), minimum capital reserves
are calculated on the basis of credit risk. Under Basel II, risk calculations
will be based in part on credit risk, market risk (i.e., adverse price move-
ments affecting the bank's portfolio of financial instruments), and operational risk.

The last component is of importance to Boards of financial institutions, since it is argued that the broad definition of operational risk, by its very nature, involves bank security, including information security. Disruptions to the use of information technology, by reason of security failures, pose both legal and functional risks, because they appear to come within the definition of operational risk.

We would suggest that, in the future, just as investors may closely scrutinize the information security of a corporation, so may its bankers. Increased attention to information security by financial institutions may have a cascading effect: as bankers increasingly guard against operational risk for capital maintenance purposes, they will increasingly consider the operational risk management of borrowers.

Transition to Basel II has created anxiety on several fronts. In the United States, for example, the Federal Deposit Insurance Corporation ("FDIC") in May 2005 expressed several concerns regarding Basel II:

> "Despite the intensive effort on Basel II development, the framework continues to produce outcomes with which supervisors are not comfortable. ... [I]mplementing risk-based capital requirements . . . could have profound competitive implications and could significantly harm the community banking sector in the U.S., as well as large non-adopters. Global banking organizations have expressed a concern about the practicality of implementing Basel II if the supervisors of individual banks around the world all insist on a bank by bank implementation of the new framework."[125]

In view of such concerns, the addition of information security to operational risk calculations contributes another element to an already volatile combination of factors to be considered by bank Boards of Directors. In short, when Directors review reports on their bank's operational risks they will be proceeding into uncharted waters, even though Directors have "significant legal and statutory mandates to ensure the safe and sound operation"[126] of their banks. As the FDIC emphasized:

> "Clearly, there is a tension between the responsibilities of individual supervisors and the cost advantages of organization-wide approaches to the implementation of Basel II. In managing this tension, the principle of absolute accountability of the management **and directors** of FDIC-insured institutions for the governance of their institutions needs to be preserved."[127]

H. Compliance with International Privacy Laws

To the extent that an organization collects, uses, or disclosures personal information in a country that has a data protection statute in place, the organization may be subject to such law. Examples include Canada's Personal Information Protection and Electronic Documents Act;[128] Australia's Privacy Act, 1988;[129] the United Kingdom's Data Protection Act, 1998;[130] and the Personal Data Protection Act of the Netherlands.[131] These comprehensive statutes, in contrast to the sectoral approach taken in the United States, require all organizations to maintain an appropriate level of security to prevent loss or theft, as well as unauthorized access, disclosure, copying, use, or modification of personal information held by the organization. The Canadian statute, for example, emphasizes a holistic approach involving physical, procedural, *and technical* security. It contains an express requirement for information security that is neutral with respect to the choice of safeguards: "Personal information shall be protected by security safeguards appropriate to the sensitivity of the information."[132] The nature of the safeguards will vary depending on the sensitivity, the amount, distribution, and format of the information, as well as it's method of storage. Also to be noted is a training requirement to ensure employees are aware of the importance of maintaining the confidentiality of personal information.[133] Because information technology has an increasingly significant role in the processing and storing of personal information, organizations need to deploy, audit, and continuously improve their information security to ensure compliance with statutory obligations for the protection of personal data.[134]

I. Compliance with Federal Trade Commission (FTC) "Fair Practices" Standards

In testimony before Congress,[135] FTC Commissioner Orson Swindle explained the FTC's belief that companies that store consumer information have a responsibility to safeguard that data to minimize the growing threat of security breaches. This should be done through the development of corporate security plans and ongoing security monitoring and oversight of operations. The FTC has brought cases under the FTC Act challenging allegedly deceptive claims by an organization concerning its information security. The FTC conducts non-public investigations of compliance with the Gramm-Leach-Bliley Act's Safeguards Rule, which, as noted earlier, requires financial institutions under the FTC's jurisdiction to implement reasonable procedures to protect consumers' personal information.

The FTC's privacy program is designed to ensure organizations keep promises they make to consumers about privacy and, in particular, the precautions they take to secure consumers' personal information. In enforcing this policy, the FTC has targeting companies that misrepresent the security of consumers' personal information. The basis for jurisdiction in each instance is that the failure to provide security commensurate with statements found in an organization's published privacy policies represents acts and practices that constitute unfair or deceptive acts, or practices in or affecting commerce, in violation of Section 5(a) of the FTC Act.[136]

To date, there are at least five FTC cases involving inadequate information security under Section 5(a) of the FTC Act: Eli Lilly (2002), Microsoft (2002), Guess.com Inc (2003), Tower Records (2004), and PETCO Animal Supplies (2004). An important lesson to draw from these cases is that each instance involved a highly sophisticated company whose misrepresentations did not occur when the company initially published its privacy and security policies. Instead, each enterprise's *practices appear to have gradually deviated from its published policies, creating discrepancies broad enough for the FTC to view those published policies as deceptive.*

These cases illustrate the need for companies to monitor and train personnel to ensure that information security goes beyond a mere statement of policy and governs conduct throughout the enterprise.[137] Submarine crews train and rehearse continuously to improve their reactions and reduce response time to threats. They do so, because every feature of equipment and every action is ultimately shaped by a concern for safety and security. Officers making decisions on board a submarine must always consider the trade-off between security/safety of the crew and the boat and achieving the mission (surveillance, weapons launch, deployment, and recovery of monitoring devices or of special forces). Similarly, each company's Directors must choose the digital protections they think most appropriate to their company and its circumstances, but the success of such efforts will turn on whether company personnel believe the digital protections are mere goals or whether instead they are requirements that everyone must meet (including Officers and Directors) in order to achieve good data governance.

FTC Cases

Eli Lily	Settled charges regarding the unauthorized disclosure of sensitive personal information
Tower Records	Settled charges that it failed to (i) implement appropriate checks and controls; (ii) adopt and implement policies and procedures to test the security of its website; and (iii) provide appropriate training and oversight for its employees, contrary to statements in its privacy policy
Guess, Inc.	Settled charges that it failed to use reasonable or appropriate measures, exposing consumers' personal information at Guess.com, including credit card numbers, to commonly known attacks by hackers, contrary to company claims
Microsoft	Settled charges regarding the privacy and security of personal information collected through its "Passport" web service, agreeing to implement a comprehensive information security program for Passport and similar services
Petco	Settled charges that it (i) failed to implement reasonable and appropriate security measures; (ii) failed to encrypt sensitive personal information; and (iii) as a result of security flaws, violated statements in its privacy policy

J. Compliance with Regulated Business Requirements

In January 2003, the telecommunications provider, Verizon-Maine ("Verizon"), sought to ensure the safety of its networks from a virus known as "the Slammer Worm" by taking its system offline for two days. This action contractually required Verizon to provide a rebate to

Competitive Local Exchange Carriers. A waiver of the monthly performance metric could be obtained, upon application, from the Maine Public Utilities Commission. This would negate the need to provide the rebates in question. Verizon filed for such waiver, claiming the attack was beyond its control and prevented it from meeting performance requirements. Verizon's application for a waiver was challenged by an allegation that it failed to take measures that would have prevented the attack. In particular, Verizon allegedly failed to apply a critical software patch issued in early October 2002 by Microsoft.

The Maine Commission concluded that Verizon "did not take all reasonable and prudent steps available to it;" although "Microsoft initially notified network administrators of a potential problem with the Slammer Worm at least six months before the attack actually occurred," and had issued security patches three months prior to the attack, Verizon chose not to install the appropriate patch.[138] The Respondents— AT&T Communications of New England and WorldCom—demonstrated that their systems were largely unaffected by the worm attack, because they had installed the Microsoft patch. Therefore, the Maine Commission determined that Verizon should be held accountable for its failure.[139]

The *Verizon-Maine* case illustrates the risk of failing to institute appropriate software patch management as part of a comprehensive approach to information security.

K. Complying with Export Control Limitations

In some circumstances, data governance also concerns certain data and technology that, while having predominantly civilian use, may also have a potential military use. Such "dual use" data and technology are subject to the Export Administration Regulations ("EAR") and cannot be exported (or re-exported) without the appropriate license from the Department of Commerce's Bureau of Industry and Security. Data and technology, which have a predominantly military use (or which have been modified for a military use) are subject to the International Traffic in Arms Regulations ("ITAR") and cannot be exported (or re-exported) without the appropriate license from the Department of State's Directorate of Defense Trade Controls. Companies having data and technology controlled by the EAR or the ITAR must ensure that they do not violate those regulations. Exports in violation of the EAR or ITAR can occur quickly with a few clicks of a mouse, transmitting controlled data and technology across the U.S. borders through the Internet.

It also should be noted that the data and technology need not cross the U.S. borders in order to be "exported" in violation of the EAR or ITAR. Both sets of regulations have what is known as "deemed export" rules. The EAR deems an export to have occurred when there is a "release of technology or source code subject to the EAR to a foreign national" in the United States, i.e., when a foreign national is shown, gains access to or comes into the possession of EAR-controlled technology or source code.[140] The controlled data or technology is deemed thereby to have been exported to the foreign national's home country. Similarly, under the ITAR, a release or export of technology is deemed to have occurred whenever there is a "[d]isclosing (including oral or visual disclosure) or transferring [of ITAR-controlled] technological data to a foreign person whether in the United States or abroad . . ."[141] Hence, companies must ensure that data controlled by the EAR or the ITAR are not shown, transferred, or made accessible to any Director, Officer, employee, or third party within the United States who is a "foreign person." Note that under the ITAR, a "foreign person" includes "any foreign corporation, business association, partnership . . . or any other entity . . . that is not incorporated or organized to do business in the United States . . . ."[142]

Since these "deemed export" rules apply also to re-exports of such data, U.S. companies that make licensed transfers of controlled data to companies in other countries must also ensure that such companies enter into agreements to abide by the EAR or ITAR controls on such data and technology. Note that although an export license issued under the EAR may include permission for re-export of the item, provided such re-export complies with all EAR requirements, no license issued under the ITAR authorizes re-export; any such re-export of an ITAR-controlled item can only be authorized by a separate license issued for that purpose.[143] U.S. companies must take particular care to ensure that such recipients understand the "deemed export" rules. The United States is one of the few countries that has a "deemed export" rule that applies to transfers of data—Canada, for example, does not have such a rule even for military data. Non-compliance with the EAR and ITAR can result in civil and criminal penalties.

A Director's fiduciary duty of care would arguably extend to ensuring that the company's data governance does not have such deficiencies that a violation of the EAR or ITAR would be "more likely than not" to occur. If, for example, in seeking to comply with SOX Section 404 a Director knew or *should have known* that deficiencies in the company's data governance made such violation "more likely than not" to occur, that would be regarded under the EAR as a "red flag" and would obligate the company (and its Directors) to conduct enhanced due diligence and to take actions necessary to preclude such violations. Directors should be aware that under a recently proposed amendment to the EAR, a U.S. person's duty to respond to a "red flag" is triggered when such person knows *or should know* that there is a "high likelihood" of a violation, and the proposed rule redefines that standard to mean that it is "more likely than not" that such violation has occurred or will occur.[144] In addition, in order to fulfill EAR and ITAR record keeping obligations, a company must maintain information security sufficient to ensure the preservation and integrity of such records.[145]

L. Complying with Contractual Requirements

Companies enter into a broad range of agreements that contain express or implicit requirements for information security or representations and warranties that such security exists and is maintained. For example, nondisclosure agreements typically contain a warranty that the recipient of proprietary information will fulfill a duty of care for such information and provide it the same high protections it provides for its own proprietary information. Similar issues arise in contracts for outsourcing and data transfers. If the recipient company, however, has no effective information security program, the company may be in breach of such warranty and, in the course of performance, such information may, as a result of such deficiencies, be compromised by or disclosed to unauthorized third parties. For these breaches, the company could be legally liable. For that reason, companies that outsource, particularly offshore,

> "should not assume that their security norms will be matched at the outsourcing candidates. ... [C]lients should require outsourcing candidates to have training programs to inform their employees of the privacy and security norms that they should apply when performing their work. These norms should reflect recognized stan-

dards. .... From a strategic perspective, clients must ensure that [outsource] candidates are on the same page (in words and meanings) with regard to their IT security objectives, strategy, and corporate security policies. .... A candidate should understand that the more sensitive the information a client entrusts to it, the more its handling of that information should be secure."[146]

Directors therefore need to verify that management has controls in place to ensure that contractual undertakings are consistent with the company's information security policies and procedures, and that company practices (and outsource vendor practices) have not diverted from, or become discrepant to, undertakings whether they be expressed in a contract or in a privacy policy.

M. Compliance with Record Retention Requirements

Data governance deserves particular attention when an enterprise has legal obligations to create and retain records. Statutes and regulations that impose such obligations continue to proliferate. Non-compliance with such record retention requirements often carries severe penalties and poses risks of reputational harm to an enterprise. Examples of such requirements include:

- *HIPAA Regulations.* Covered entities must retain records for six years relating to any disclosure of electronic protected health information.[147]
- *ITAR:* Any enterprise that manufactures, modifies, or exports defense articles must maintain records concerning such articles' "manufacture, acquisition and disposition" for a period of five years from the expiration of the applicable license or other approval.[148]
- *SEC Regulations.* Every member of a national security exchange and every broker or dealer is required "to preserve for a period of not less than six years, the first two years in an accessible place,"[149] all records specified in regulations issued by the SEC, and if an enterprise elects to preserve such records in "electronic storage media" such media must, among other requirements, "Preserve the records in a non-rewritable, non-eraseable format."[150]

Therefore, Directors need to ensure that management has appropriate policies and procedures in place to achieve such compliance (and that it has not deemed such compliance a mere "housekeeping" matter that it assumes will be handled without diligent monitoring).

N. Complying with "Litigation Hold" Orders and Averting Spoliation of Evidence

Recent "corporate scandals" have resulted in enforcement agencies, prosecutors, and litigation counsel giving increased attention to failures to preserve discoverable and relevant evidence, particularly electronically stored information. Such information will be found on a company's computers and portable electronic devices, as well as on backup tapes and other forms of long-term storage. However, unless companies plan long in advance to protect electronic records when they incur legal obligations to do so, they may find themselves in breach of such obligations because their information technology systems have continuously been destroying such records. As commentators explain:

> "A problem with discovering electronic data, however, is that it is much more susceptible to unintentional destruction than hard copy documents. Electronic data is often recycled or overwritten as part of normal business practices because a business cannot or need not retain large volumes of outdated information. When litigation ensures, companies need to take affirmative steps to prevent the destruction of certain relevant electronic documents, such as e-mails, computer records, and possibly back-up tapes. Not surprisingly, spoliation has become a significant e-discovery problem, . . ."[151]

Claims of spoliation of evidence—the destruction or significant alteration of evidence, or the failure to preserve property for another's use as evidence in pending or reasonably foreseeable litigation[152]—used to be a rare occurrence in enforcement actions and lawsuits. Recently, however, there have been numerous decisions of spoliation cases just in the Second Circuit (which includes the federal courts in the State of New York).[153] Many of these cases involve failures to preserve electronically stored information, particularly internal and external emails. The cases also often involve (i) failures by company personnel to follow guidance issued by their own legal counsel to fulfill the duty to protect relevant electronic evidence and (ii) failures to recognize how early that duty attaches.

The duty to preserve arises once a party knows or *reasonably should know* that information is: (i) relevant to anticipated or pending action; (ii) reasonably calculated to lead to the discovery of admissible evidence; (iii) reasonably likely to be requested during discovery; or (iv) the subject of a pending discovery request.[154]

Most U.S. companies attempt to reduce their litigation risk (and storage costs) by establishing a routine destruction of old records, obsolete files, and other unnecessary information through "document retention" programs. When a company anticipates litigation or an investigation, and thereby incurs a duty to preserve relevant electronically stored information, its duty includes the issuance of what is referred to as a "litigation hold" order to all personnel, including Officers and Directors. A "litigation hold" is an order identifying the scope of relevant information to the anticipated litigation and directing all personnel to take affirmative steps to ensure that all such information is preserved.

In practice, this means personnel are to cease deleting any files related to the matter and ensure that automated backups, recycling, overwriting, and other computer routines are comprehensively adjusted or halted to preserve all such relevant, electronically stored information *in its original condition.* Fulfillment of such duty often becomes quite burdensome. Nonetheless, the duty must be fulfilled every day until the "litigation hold" is lifted, which should not occur until the case is settled or decided (including final disposition of all appeals).

If a company suffers a breakdown in its information security during a period when it is under an obligation to have implemented a "litigation hold" it may find that information and records it was obligated to preserve have thereby been damaged, destroyed, or rendered all but irretrievable except at exorbitant expense. A company that maintains weak information security procedures will probably also find it difficult to prove that an information security breach caused such damage or loss, and even if it can carry that burden of proof, it may then find itself confronted with allegations that its information security reflected an indifference to its duties to preserve potentially relevant information and records.[155]

The consequences in litigation may be substantial fines and/or an "adverse inference" instruction to a jury or, in extreme cases, entry of a default judgment.[156] For example, in July 2004, a United States Magistrate Judge (in the Northern District of Ohio, Eastern Division) recommended that the District Court enter default judgment on liability against PricewaterhouseCooper, LLP ("PwC") and in favor of Telxon

Corporation and class action plaintiffs, because as the Judge explained, PwC failed to properly preserve its electronic records:

> "PwC failed at the start of discovery to check thoroughly its local servers and its archives for relevant documents, failed to compare the various versions of relevant documents on those databases, failed to produce documents as they were kept in the ordinary course of business, and failed to reproduce thoroughly and accurately all documents and their attachments. Prior to litigation PwC had permitted destruction of documents despite committing to their preservation. Despite these failures, PwC time and time again told the court and the parties that it had made a complete disclosure of all relevant documents and attachments and that it had produced them in the order in which they were stored by PwC. The only conclusion that the court can reach is that PwC and/or its counsel engaged in deliberate fraud or was so recklessly indifferent to their responsibilities as a party to the litigation that they failed to take the most basic steps to fulfill those responsibilities."[157]

More recently, in the high profile case of *Coleman (Parent) Holdings, Inc. v. Morgan Stanley & Co., Inc.* (in which plaintiff sued the defendant Morgan Stanley for fraud), Judge Elizabeth Maass granted plaintiff's motion for an adverse inference instruction to the jury in response to defendant's failure to fulfill its affirmative duty to produce its e-mails, its noncompliance with federal law requiring it to preserve e-mails, its certification that it had produced all e-mails required (which proved untrue and which certification the defendant withdrew on the eve of trial), and its failure after 12 months to comply with the Court's order to conduct proper searches and produce e-mails responsive to plaintiff's discovery request.[158] Judge Maass issued an adverse inference instruction to the jury (that the jury could assume the defendant bank had aided and abetted in the defrauding of the plaintiff—and that defendant thus had the burden of persuading the jury that the defendant did not conspire to defraud the plaintiff).[159] The jury eventually returned a verdict for plaintiff and awarded it $604 million in damages[160] and $850 million in punitive damages.[161] These two cases (*PwC* and *Morgan Stanley*) are not isolated incidents, and what has been noted in the *Financial Times* of the *Morgan Stanley* case was reflected also in the *PricewaterhouseCoopers* case, namely that it "highlights the dangers that companies face when dealing with large quantities of email evidence involved in lawsuits."[162]

The consequences in the context of a government agency investigation are comparably severe and may be incurred more unexpectedly because the threshold for violations is much lower and because an official proceeding need not be pending or about to be instituted for a violation to occur.[163] The consequences can include obstruction of justice charges and, if convicted, long-term imprisonment.[164] Note, for example, that SOX, Section 1519 makes it a criminal offense for anyone who "knowingly alters, destroys, mutilates, conceals, covers up, falsifies, or makes a false entry in any record, document, or tangible object with the intent to impede, obstruct, or influence the investigation or proper administration of any matter within the jurisdiction of any department or agency of the United States . . . ," and for each such violation a person can be fined, or imprisoned up to 20 years, or both.[165]

O. Key Points and Priority Issues

The developing law pertaining to data governance suggests that Directors should devote increased attention to the subject because material weaknesses or deficiencies in data governance could result in noncompliance with applicable laws or breach of duties.

Our review of legal "drivers" suggests that the following be among the priorities that Directors should pursue in their data governance discussions with management:

- the company's data governance policies and procedures (particularly the framework surrounding access to sensitive information);
- the company's information systems;
- the company's information security risk assessments;
- the lines of authority and responsibility for data governance (particularly for responses to breaches in security and attempted breaches);
- the company's policies and procedures for creation and retention of records, and for ensuring, in the event of anticipated litigation or government investigation, that all relevant records are preserved unchanged as of the date the company or its counsel issue a "hold" order; and
- the company's "tripwires" when corporate activities trigger additional compliance requirements for information security.

To pursue those priorities, Directors need a "tactical picture," which they can develop by using the materials this Guide provides in the next Chapter.

CHAPTER 4

View Through the Periscope: Questions for Board Members to Pose to Management

This Chapter is intended to help Directors decide what lines of inquiry to pursue with management in order to understand their company's data governance environment. It provides them with questions to open and illuminate those inquiries. It is also intended to help Directors discern when their questions and concerns about information security have not been adequately answered or addressed. For that purpose we provide brief "commentary" to assist Directors in assessing the answers received from management. And, in instances where we think Directors may overlook an issue due to differentials in experience or expertise, we highlight as "red flags" potential weaknesses or deficiencies in digital protection or security.

A Director's immediate reaction to the subject of data governance might be to ask if there is a "problem," and then to ask "what are we doing?" These are legitimate questions but will probably generate uninformative answers. Questions such as "how do we learn of new threats or vulnerabilities to our information security?" or "how do we learn if our information systems have been penetrated or compromised?" are more detailed but are still limited even with this specificity. Directors, in keeping with their mandate and fiduciary responsibilities, should focus primarily on "systemic" policy, operational, and audit questions that enable them to understand and oversee their organization's data governance.

The objective is to develop a good level of data governance that Directors, in exercise of their business judgment, determine to be commensurate with the value and sensitivity of the organization's information assets. To achieve that objective, Directors need to construct a dynamic "tactical mosaic"—regularly updated using formal reviews with management, supplemented with reports that personnel will be encouraged to route directly to the relevant senior officer and revised in the event of a serious security incident or the emergence of a new and dangerous threat.

The initial snapshot of the tactical mosaic should be of the organization's business context, enabling Directors to identify the organization's critical business assets. The next snapshot should be of the organization's data governance, enabling Directors to identify the probable risks to the critical information assets and the gaps in the organization's defensive measures for protection of those assets. The resulting mosaic, representing the combination of these two snapshots, should provide Directors with a grasp of the information assets at stake, the risks and threats to such assets, the strengths and weaknesses in the company's protective measures and the additional measures in which it should consider investing, e.g., enhanced training of personnel, improved security procedures and deployment of defensive technologies.

To guide Directors in the development of their "tactical mosaic," we propose practical questions, arranged in four broad categories, for Directors to consider using as points of departure for discussions with management.

- Policies and Procedures
- Organizational Measures
- Assessments and Updates
- Mitigation and Response to Security Incidents

Our approach, that of proposing questions for Directors to put to senior management as a way of gaining insight into their performance in order to oversee it, is consistent with that adopted by the Office of Inspector General of the U.S. Department of Health and Human Services in a 2003 guide for health care organization Directors.[166] The commentary represents commonly accepted security practices readily recommended by security practitioners and documented in codes and standards such as ISO 17799, the National Institute of Standards and Technology's publications *Computer Security* and *Information Security* and the Carnegie Mellon Software Engineering Institute's *Capability Maturity Model Integration*.

Directors should note that the deliberate brevity of this Guide allowed only the highest priority topics to be addressed. Thus this Guide is not exhaustive, but indicates key questions that Directors should ask and which provide initial direction and terms of reference for their discussion with senior management concerning the data governance policies, practices, and procedures of the organization.

A. Policies and Planning

1. Have we adopted and documented an Information Security Policy, and how do we enforce it?

Construction of a "tactical mosaic" starts with an understanding of what policy, if any, the organization has in place for its information security. The policy should be documented. It should both establish security objectives and priortize those objectives to be achieved in the current reporting period. The implementation of the policy should be set forth in a "security procedures" document that delineates the practices that all personnel (including Officers and Directors) must adhere to as security requirements. Each person should know what security conduct is required of them, both in daily practice (do's and don'ts) and in response to security breaches or other threats to information assets (their role in emergency response and damage control). These documents should communicate to managers and employees the organization's commitment and approach to managing information security. Gaps in any such policy or inconsistencies discerned between policy and practices will provide an immediate agenda with short and medium term objectives.

Answer Assessment: An absence of such a policy represents a critical error on the part of the organization. The existence of a policy and implementing procedures should reflect recognition of the importance of information security. The quality of such policy and procedures will depend, in part, on whether they define the organization's security principles, standards, and compliance requirements, and the consequences of security policy violations. It addition, they should establish general and specific responsibilities for information security management, including the reporting of security incidents.

2. Have we developed a set of business continuity plans to address a range of disruptive scenarios?

In the Digital Era, the continuity of an organization's business operations depends foremost on the performance of its information technology systems. Any breach of security that dampens the performance of such systems will severely diminish the tempo of business operations. Most Directors understand that link and dependency, but nonetheless underestimate the amplified effects on business operations that seemingly small disruptions can cause. As a result, "worst case" scenarios and the continuity plans that address them often overlook the ways that minor problems, when misunderstood, can spiral into catastrophic information technology events.[167] Business continuity management should include controls to identify and minimize a broad range of risks, limit the consequences of damaging incidents, and ensure the timely resumption of essential operations, especially the early resumption of information technology system operations. They should also specify the conditions for activating such plans, the procedures to be followed, and actions to be taken. The objective is to ensure that critical business processes can be restored within specified timeframes.

Answer Assessment: The existence of only one business continuity plan is probably insufficient. If the organization has not reviewed and modified its business continuity plans in response to serious security incidents or significant changes in information technology systems, they are undoubtedly obsolete. The sufficiency of management's response will depend on whether it has ensured that the business continuity plans reflect the organization's processes and structure, and place priority of recovery on critical business processes. Management should make clear whether its assessment of risks and threats include any that could damage critical information assets and to which the organization is particularly vulnerable or lacks adequate safeguards. Directors should assess management's business continuity strategy and the documentation of such plans. They should consider asking management to walk them through a minimum of two "worst case scenarios" to explain how the continuity plans would give personnel the guidance they need to preserve continuity (if it is jeopardized) and to recover it (if it is interrupted). Business continuity plans may include consideration of the purchase of insurance.

3. Have we established a record retention policy?

As its name suggests, a record retention policy should address the retention and disposal of documents, records, information (including information in digital form), and electronic storage media. The FTC has cautioned, "there are few foolproof methods of record destruction."[168] The policy, therefore, should be quite specific about the measures to ensure secure disposal of all digital media. The policy should also make clear when circumstances require that the retention program be suspended through issuance to all personnel of a "litigation hold" order.

Answer assessment: Absence of a record retention policy, or omission of procedures for its timely and enforced suspension, represents errors by the organization. If no suspension policy exists, then Directors may wish to request management, in consultation with counsel, to draft a "litigation hold and preservation plan" so that the company will have it when it needs it, i.e., when the company reasonably "foresees" that certain actions or activities will probably result in a government investigation or in litigation.

If such policies exist, their quality will depend on whether, at a minimum, they provide guidelines on the retention, storage, handling, and disposal of records and information; ways to monitor and enforce those guidelines; and, if they contain a retention schedule, identification of essential record types and the period of time for which such records should be retained. In addition to business practicalities, such retention periods should recognize legal requirements for long-term preservation of records (e.g., HIPAA, OSHA, EAR, and ITAR each impose long-term record preservation requirements). The record retention policy should indicate what controls have been implemented to protect essential records, documents, and information from unauthorized destruction. Such policies may indicate a "red flag" if they do not include regularly scheduled training, particularly in the disposal of sensitive digital records and the strict adherence to a "litigation hold" order when issued. Management should be asked if they have consulted with legal counsel on this issue, the advice received, and the extent to which it has been followed.

4. Have we established a privacy policy?

Personal information is often a subset of the information held by the organization. Specific legislative requirements, both domestic and international, concerning privacy and data protection may apply to the organization. If the organization outsources business processing operations offshore to countries that have privacy laws or onshore to states that have enacted personal data protection statutes, the organization's privacy policies and procedures should reflect the need to comply with such legal requirements.

Answer assessment: Absence of such a policy represents a gap in the organization's data governance. If such policy exists, its quality will depend on whether, at a minimum, it outlines the purpose for any collection, use, or disclosure of personal information; addresses the subjects of consent, unauthorized access, and incident reporting obligations (if any); and indicates that access and complaint handling mechanisms exist. The more comprehensive an organization's privacy policy, written in a manner to be clearly understood by the reader, the more likely it will be considered in compliance with transparency principles found in voluntary privacy codes or in legislative requirements.

A privacy policy represents only one aspect of a "privacy compliance program" and supplemental questions about the organization's management of personal information and the vulnerability of such information to unauthorized access may be of interest to Directors at another time. Directors should ask management to verify that the organization's privacy policy (or policies) and any published privacy statement have been carefully compared and are consistent with each other and with current practices by organizational personnel.

B. Organizational Measures

1. Have we established accountability for data governance?

There are a number of aspects to consider in assessing any answer to this question. First, data governance, especially with respect to information security, is a business responsibility that should be a "shared responsibility" among all members of an organization's management. A "multi-disciplinary" approach to data governance should be encouraged. Depending on which aspects are under consideration, this will involve managers, business unit leaders, computer system users, administrators, application designers, auditors, security staff, as well as legal counsel, insurers, and risk managers.

Second, specific responsibilities for data governance may form part of the job description of an individual. The placement of responsibility will vary but not the function. Whether this is a Chief Information Officer in a large organization or a network administrator in a small one, care should be taken to ensure that conflicts of interest in responsibilities (i.e., operations and security) are avoided. Management must ensure that "someone" with clearly defined authority is assigning roles and co-coordinating the implementation of data management security throughout the organization. This function needs to be supported by a Board or senior management committee dedicated to ensuring data governance policies are in place and monitoring whether an appropriate level of corporate resources has been dedicated.

Answer Assessment: Determining whether accountability has been established will depend first on whether job descriptions of key personnel include a data management or security component, second on whether a person has been assigned specific responsibilities (e.g., monitoring significant changes in the "threat environment," reviewing and/ or managing security incidents), and third on whether management has instituted a "cross-organizational" group to recommend major initiatives for the enhancement of good data governance within the organization. Provision should also be made for review and recommendation of changes in policy and responsibilities, and for the promotion of data governance initiatives, e.g., awareness programs.

2. Have we addressed the data governance aspects of our third party relationships?

Whether formalized through comprehensive "outsourcing" arrangements or simply the employment of external resources for specific assignments, the use of third parties requires consideration of that party's data governance and its handling of the organization's information.

In some jurisdictions (e.g., Europe, Canada) or sectors (e.g., health, financial institutions), accountability for information remains with the "collecting" organization, despite the onward transfer to service providers or partners.[169]

Access may be physical (e.g., to offices, filing cabinets) or electronic (e.g. to databases, information systems) and may involve access to the organization's systems or the provision of information by the organization.

Answer assessment: The adequacy of management's response to this question will depend on whether it indicates that (i) a thorough inventory of third party relationships has been made, (ii) all relevant agreements/memoranda of understanding have been reviewed, and (iii) the subject of information protection has been addressed in each instance. Such agreements, at a minimum, should require compliance with security and privacy policies and standards as well as specific restrictions on use and access.

3. Have we categorized our information holdings according to the sensitivity of the information?

The categorization of information need not be an extensive undertaking but should reflect need for security, priorities, and degree of protection as well as consider the organization's business needs to share or restrict access to information. While less sensitive information **generally** means less intense security requirements, this may not be the case where "brand" or "image" is in play. For example, if a test environment at a government department was hacked, the news report may not indicate that it was a test system, rather that it was simply a government system that was affected.

Answer Assessment: The lack of information categorization represents a material deficiency. Failure to categorize information means that employees will not be sufficiently cognizant of the sensitivity of the information they handle and distribute and will be at heightened risk of granting other personnel or third parties inappropriate access to sensitive information.

If information is categorized, then the sufficiency of categorization should reflect that it is a dynamic process: what was sensitive yesterday may not be so in six months—and *vice versa*. The applicable legal requirements should be reflected in categorizations (e.g., any data that is EAR-controlled or ITAR-controlled must be categorized to preclude access to such information by foreign nationals where the requisite license for such access has not been obtained from the U.S. government). Any categorizing procedures must be periodically reviewed.

4. Have we allocated information access through a formal authorization process?

Inappropriate use of access privileges is often found to be a major factor in security breaches. Limiting access to information on an "as required"/"as needed" basis protects against unauthorized access and/or disclosure. The periodic review of access rights should be part of any authorization process. There should also be strict procedures in place for restriction or denial of access to personnel who are known to be leaving the organization.

Answer assessment: The absence of access or privilege management controls represents a critical error in management. Where an access control system exists, the adequacy of such a system will depend upon whether the privileges associated with each system and application, and the categories of staff to which they need to be allocated, have been identified and whether such privileges are allocated on a need-to-use or event-by-event basis. Good data governance would include adherence to this "principle of least privilege." Similarly, management should provide a description of the authorization process, which should include a record system showing the allocation of privileges and checks to ensure that privileges are not granted until the authorization process is complete and, that when personnel no longer have a "need to use" the system or a restricted data base, that their access privileges are terminated immediately.

5. Have we appropriately segregated all job responsibilities associated with information and information security?

Segregation of the management or execution of certain duties or responsibilities should minimize accidental or deliberate system misuse. Segregation ultimately means the involvement of two or more people in critical areas of activity or control so as to ensure a division of responsibilities, and denies any single individual the opportunity to exploit his or her access to tamper with the system or the information it holds. As an example of the importance of this concept, segregation of duties is one of the specific areas that the GAO checked when it audited information system controls in 2004 at the Federal Deposit Insurance Corporation.[170]

Small organizations may find the segregation of security responsibilities challenging in practice, but the principle of segregating security and audit functions from operational duties should be adopted. If such segregation is difficult, given the size of the organization, consideration should be given to segregating control activities.

Answer assessment: Directors assessing the adequacy of management's response to this question will need to be satisfied as to whether any individual (at any level) can perpetrate fraud, theft, or mischief without being promptly detected. They should also ascertain that the organization does not permit all network users to have unrestricted "read access" to sensitive information and that restrictions are in place on who is permitted to perform maintenance and repair activities. An often-overlooked vulnerability is on-site, third party service providers such as programmers and other information technology professionals. Provision should be made for the supervision of their activities to prevent introduction into the information technology system of unauthorized changes to application and system software.[171]

6. Have we been conducting sufficient training of employees with respect to data governance policies and procedures?

Security training helps ensure that employees are aware of information security threats and concerns and are equipped to support the organization's security policy. Record management training helps ensure compliance with litigation hold orders. Education, when combined with ongoing communications, helps strengthen employee awareness of data governance. Training, however, should conspicuously include Officers and Directors, to ensure their compliance, to lead by example, and to send a message of the importance of adhering to data policies and procedures. It should ensure that, comparable to training of a submarine crew, everyone can capably perform their assigned responsibilities in the harsh and unforgiving environment in which the organization operates.

Answer assessment: The sufficiency of management's response will depend on whether it (i) indicates that such training occurs with appropriate frequency, scope, and depth; (ii) confirms that qualified personnel conduct it; (iii) ensures that there are timely updates (particularly when applicable legal requirements have changed); and (iv) demonstrates that the organization uses clear means to communicate such updates to employees, Officers, and Directors.

A further consideration is the content of such training, which should include an explanation of data governance requirements, legal responsibilities, and business controls. Any audit should also test to verify whether training has resulted in equipping personnel to safeguard the information technology systems and to respond and report, as needed, in the event of security incidents or emergencies involving the information technology systems or information assets.

7. Have we put in place change management mechanisms for our information systems?

Inadequate control of changes to information systems is a common cause of system failures or security breaches. An organization's information security procedures should include formal change management responsibilities and formal supervised steps to ensure control of any change to equipment, software or procedures.

Answer assessment: The adequacy of management's response will depend on whether such mechanisms exist, their rigor, and whether they are reasonably designed to prevent tampering with information systems. If they do not exist, this raises concerns about management's control of the organization's information systems. If they exist, the sufficiency of the mechanisms will depend on certain minimum requirements. For example, they should require the identification and recording of all significant changes and assessments before implementation to measure the potential impact of such changes. Similarly, a formal approval procedure for proposed changes should exist as well as procedures to abort or recover from unsuccessful changes. Consideration has to be given to ensuring the communication of changes solely to persons who "need to know" of them.

Directors should consider becoming familiar with two important metrics: What percentage of systems generate audit trails that provide a trace of user actions? What percentage of systems *that store sensitive data* generate such audit trails? If the answers are not satisfactory, it indicates a "red flag" because the other measures might not be sufficient to achieve prompt detection of unauthorized access.

C. Assessments and Updates

1. Does our organization have mechanisms to regularly update security measures?

It is anticipated that risks to an organization's information assets will continue to increase. Organizations that do not update their security measures increase the probability that their safeguards will become obsolete and leave the organization's information assets increasingly vulnerable.

Answer assessment: The adequacy of management's response to this question will depend, in part, on whether it conducts ongoing and regularly scheduled reviews of its security measures. Such updates should be coordinated with the audits of the organization's data governance to ensure that new vulnerabilities are promptly identified and measures diligently applied to reduce the organization's exposure.

2. Are our information systems regularly and independently audited for compliance with security standards?

Technical compliance audits involve the examination of operational systems to ensure that hardware and software controls have been correctly implemented. Compliance audits should also involve reconnaissance testing (to detect surveillance that may be a prelude to a cyber-attack), vulnerability assessments and penetration testing (to determine what vulnerabilities exist, and whether the system and monitoring personnel can promptly detect and properly react to intrusions).

Answer assessment: The adequacy of management's response to this question will depend on whether audit requirements have been defined and accepted by the relevant business managers (keeping in mind their responsibilities also involve a security element) and whether all procedures, requirements, and responsibilities are documented. Similarly, all access to information systems should be monitored and logged to produce a reference trail.

Sufficient resources for performing audits or system checks should be identified and made available.

At a minimum, audits should be conducted annually and access to system audit tools should be restricted. If the organization's personnel involved in information technology operations conduct the audits, this could create a false sense of security by reason of a breakdown in the segregation of duties and the possible concealment of misconduct by personnel. If the organization outsources key information technology system functions or information processing, the audits should extend to the third party providers.

3. Do we have mechanisms to ensure periodic, independent review of data governance measures?

The data governance policy and procedures of any organization requires periodic, independent review to provide assurance that organizational practices properly reflect the policy, and that the policy is feasible and effective. Such reviews also permit an organization to become aware of emerging threats and vulnerabilities, as well as best practices in controls and counter-measures.

Answer assessment: Management's response to this question should be affirmative. This review could form part of the internal audit function, or be conducted by a third party organization specializing in such reviews. A further consideration is whether the findings of such reviews are satisfactorily addressed and what resources management has committed to improving the organization's data governance, and specifically its information security. On this last point, the U.S. General Accounting Office provides good guidance:

> "To ensure an effective test and evaluation program, security management best practices prescribe that the scope of information sys-

tem control tests include an evaluation of recently identified weaknesses and an assessment of emerging security threats to the computer control environment. ... [S]elf-assessment processes [should] include[ ] provisions for updating ... annual review of information system controls to evaluate control weaknesses that were identified in prior audits."[172]

An effective security program also extends to those who perform such testing or assessments. As the Federal Financial Institutions Examination Council cautions: "Because testing may uncover nonpublic customer information, appropriate safeguards to protect the information must be in place."[173]

4. Do we conduct security reviews of every new technology that is introduced formally by management or informally by personnel into the organization?

The introduction of new technologies almost invariably introduces unsuspected vulnerabilities. The problem occurs whether management authorizes the introduction (e.g., a VoIP system or WiMax[174]) or personnel introduce a new technology on their own initiative (e.g., instant messaging).

Answer assessment: Omission of a policy to conduct checks for introduction of new technologies or for security risks is a material deficiency. Directors should expect management to make such security reviews a high priority and an integral part of any decision to invest in new technology. Such reviews should also reflect management's awareness and use of reputable reports of security risks in such technologies and best counter-measures (e.g., FDIC guidance on instant messaging,[175] GAO cautions concerning wireless technologies,[176] and vendor white papers and NIST studies on VoIP security[177]).

Management of public companies should ensure that, in accordance with recommendations by the SEC's staff, the organization test and assess any new technology's potential impact on internal controls so that the organization will prepare "reliable financial statements following the implementation" of a new technology or information system.[178]

D. Mitigation and Response to Security Breaches

1. Have we established incident management procedures?

Procedures should be considered for any type of incident but should expressly address: information system failures and loss of service; denial of service; errors resulting from incomplete or inaccurate business data; and breaches of confidentiality.

Answer assessment: The absence of such procedures represents an area of concern. Management's response to this question will not be satisfactory unless they indicate that such procedures exist and address such topics as: the analysis and identification of the cause of the incident; the planning and implementation of remedies to prevent recurrence; the collection of audit trails and similar evidence; communication with those affected by, or involved with, recovery from the incident; prompt reporting of the incident to the appropriate authorities; and alerting third parties in the event that the consequences resulting from the incident might cause damage to others.

2. Do we have incident reporting procedures in place?

There are two main uses of such mechanisms: to minimize the damage from incidents and to learn from them.

Answer assessment: While procedures need not be complicated, they should exist and evidence that management has made all employees and contractors aware of the procedures for the prompt reporting of different types of incidents (e.g., security breach, inadvertent disclosure, emerging threat, identified weakness, or malfunction).[179]

3. Do we have a formal disciplinary process for dealing with employees or contractors who commit policy or procedural breaches?

Even if rarely invoked, such a process can act as a deterrent to employees or contractors who may otherwise disregard data governance policies or procedures. Moreover, it is a necessary component for an effective legal compliance program, omission of which would provide enforcement agencies and potential plaintiffs grounds for alleging negligence or reckless indifference with respect to security duties and breaches.

Answer assessment: Directors should expect management to indicate that the organization's formal disciplinary process for employees covers those who violate organizational data governance policies and procedures and that this has been communicated to all employees.

Similarly, management should indicate that contracts with contractors or third party service providers address the subject of data governance and permit the organization to consider appropriate enforceable remedies, up to and including termination of the contract, in the event of a breach of policy or procedures.

CHAPTER 5

Conclusion

"[P]iloting becomes another matter when you apply it to vast streams like the Mississippi and the Missouri, whose alluvial banks cave and change constantly, whose snags are always hunting up new quarters, whose sand-bars are never at rest, whose channels are for ever dodging and shirking, and whose obstructions must be confronted in all nights and all weathers without the aid of a single light-house or a single buoy . . . in all this three or four thousand miles of villainous river."
—Mark Twain, *Life on the Mississippi*

In today's competitive business environment, organizations have limited resources and tend to focus on improving only information security, and then only to the extent that security measures appear necessary to continue their business operations or are demanded by stakeholders. This Guide has sought to demonstrate that the topic of data governance has an intrinsic importance that goes beyond a risk-of-investment calculation. Data governance, and its subsets of information security and data privacy, should be considered an "infrastructure" cost that limits extrinsic business risks and averts what may become catastrophic "crisis" events. While Directors need to address the issue, it is important to note that data governance involves risk management not risk avoidance. "Bad things" do happen to "good people"—the objective in any organization is to minimize such events.

It must also be remembered that data governance represents a continuous process rather than periodic decision-making. Management has to ensure that the structure and operations of the organization can be vigilant against evolving threats or vulnerabilities by monitoring and adapting technology, procedures and policies, all with the view to updating the organization's readiness to withstand possible attacks. Directors need to ensure that management does this.

Data governance requires integration or, more precisely, the integrated management of risk using a variety of mechanisms. In a particular situation, physical and/or procedural requirements may complement the security provided by technology. Digital risks are not the only risks to consider, since much of an organization's data continues to be stored in hard copy. Although external risks from the Internet and new technologies are increasing, technology alone should not be perceived as a quick, permanent, or comprehensive fix. There is no substitute for good data governance and its implementation by management in the day-to-day operations of any organization.

The reader should not consider this Guide as conveying any general suggestion that management ignores information security. On the contrary, in the United Kingdom, nearly eight out of ten companies rate security as the single most important attribute of corporate networks, according to new research. Similarly, a poll of 254 senior executives by the Economist Intelligence Unit found that security has replaced network reliability and availability as the most critical network attribute. The report also noted that network security spending outpaced overall information technology expenditures. Organizationally, the chief executive is taking ownership of network security policy in some companies, while in others a relatively new role, that of chief security officer, is emerging.[180]

Directors who read this Guide are encouraged to review existing data governance measures and to ensure they are effective given the organization's business environment and risk tolerance. To the extent that they do, this modest Guide has achieved a worthy degree of success.

Endnotes

1. Information security and data privacy each contain, in turn, important subsets. Information security includes risk assessment, threat deterrence and detection, defensive counter-measures, and response-and-recovery procedures. Data privacy includes availability, access integrity, and data retention.

2. As the *Financial Times* has reported:

> "Recent years have seen a dramatic increase in board-level recognition of the importance of corporate security policies in securing both physical and intellectual assets—and ultimately safeguarding shareholder value. According to the Institute of Chartered Accountants in England & Wales and The Risk Advisory Group, more than half of all companies now report that they review [information security] risks at every board meeting or once a quarter."

Sarah Murray, *Facing a New World of Risk*, FINANCIAL TIMES, July 14, 2004, Special Section Understanding Corporate Security, p. 3. And as *The Economist* more recently observed:

> "The issue of data protection has . . . ceased to be a topic left to geeks in the computer department. These days it is a matter for chief executives and their boards of directors in almost every type of business . . ."

Hot Data, THE ECONOMIST, June 25–July 1, 2005, p. 15.

3. A recent survey by Ernst and Young reflect several "disconnects" among executive officers, which presumably are shared by the Directors who oversee them. Security is rated important, but does not receive a budget commensurate with its attributed priority. The top security concern among officers was major viruses, Trojans, or Internet worms, even though internal risks are a more serious problem. And security aware-

ness still receives more lip service than the extensive and recurrent training needed to ensure that personnel implement digital protections effectively. See Conrath, Chris, *Survey Reveals a Security Disconnect*, COMPUTERWORLD, October 21, 2004, accessed at http://www.computerworld.com.au/index.php/id;96671287; relcomp;1.

4. As noted by the International Chamber of Commerce ("ICC"), "Private businesses own and operate most of the world's information systems and infrastructure. They therefore have a clear responsibility to the overall development and promotion of information security. This needs to be understood at the highest levels of companies." ICC, SECURING YOUR BUSINESS, July 2004, p. 12, accessed at http://www.iccwbo.org/home/e_business/RESOURCES-rev4.pdf.

5. As noted by a London computer security firm, Mi2g Ltd., "in February 2004 alone, Mi2g estimates, various malevolent attacks caused upwards of $68 billion in damages worldwide, much of it due to worms, such as MyDoom and several others that rampaged through the Internet that month" and from just the SQL Slammer worm Mi2g estimated the amount of damages to be "about US $1 billion. . .related mostly to lost productivity." Riordan, James, Wespi, Andreas, and Zamboni, Diego, *How to Hook Worms*, IEEE SPECTRUM, May 2005, p. 33.

6. Note also the historical perspective provided by members of the Information Services and Technology Group at Intel:

> "Computer networks and computing infrastructure have evolved from a static, one-dimensional, and physically connected model to a dynamic, multidimensional, and virtual model. This evolution, along with the growing threat of more sophisticated and dynamically adjusting exploits and attacks, has resulted in significant challenges to the ability of the IT infrastructure to provide essential services in the presence of attacks and failures as well as to recover to full services in a timely manner (survivability), and to the ability for network computing systems to provide users with services as intended without compromising service integrity, user privacy, and data confidentiality (trustworthiness)."

Brown, Gardos, Hopman, Li, Loucheheim, Pickering, Sedayao, and Vicente, *The Proactive Enterprise*, INTEL TECHNOLOGY JOURNAL, November 2004, p. 262.

7. Killingsworth, Scott, *observation in e-mail to authors, May 30, 2005.*

8. Trope, Roland L. and Upchurch, Greg, CHECKPOINTS IN CYBERSPACE, American Bar Association, 2005, p. 349.

9. "Every year corporations and government installations spend millions of dollars fortifying their network infrastructures. Firewalls, intrusion detection systems, and antivirus products stand guard at network boundaries, and individuals monitor countless logs and sensors from even the subtlest hints of network penetration. . . . [B]ut very few technological measures exist to guard against insiders—those entities that operate *inside* the fortified network boundary. The 2002 CSI/FBI survey estimates that 70 percent of successful attacks come from the inside."

Thompson, Herbert H., *Security Perfect Storm?*, ACM QUEUE, June 2004, p. 59.

10. Huband, Mark, *Uneven Levels of Preparedness*, FINANCIAL TIMES FT CORPORATE SECURITY, May 10, 2004, p. 1.

11. Internal risks come from carelessness as well as malice. One security expert clearly explains the latter risk:

"A malicious insider is a dangerous and insidious adversary. He's already inside the system he wants to attack, so he can ignore any perimeter defenses around the system. He probably has a high level of access, and could be considered trusted by the system he is attacking. . . . Insiders can be impossible to stop because they're the exact same people you're forced to trust. . . . Insiders are not necessarily employees. They can be consultants and contractors. . . . Most computer security measures—firewalls, intrusion detection systems . . . try to deal with the external attacker, but are pretty much powerless against insiders. Insiders might be less likely to attack a system than outsiders are, but systems are *far more vulnerable to them*. An insider knows how the systems work and where the weak points are . . . and *how any investigation against his actions would be conducted.*

. . .

Cyberspace is particularly susceptible to insiders, because it is rife with insider knowledge. The person who writes a security program can put a back door in it. The person who installs a firewall can leave a secret opening. The person whose job it is to audit a security system can deliberately overlook a few things."

Schneier, Bruce, SECRETS & LIES, John Wiley & Sons, Inc., 2000, pp. 47–48 and 265.

Carelessness should be perceived not merely as a risk from low-ranked personnel or external parties granted access, but also as a risk from senior personnel, who are ultimately responsible for enforcing digital security, monitoring it, and setting the top-down example. When the head of the Central Intelligence Agency carelessly granted himself permission to violate agency rules against downloading secrets into personal laptops and taking them off-premises and into the home, he amply illustrated the risks from senior officials who let themselves believe they are above the rules intended for everyone. Any rule with such exceptions poses a severe security risk, and organizations must always be alert to persons who grant themselves exceptions that no one should receive.

12. "Educational and awareness programs are one of the most important (and one of the most frequently under-supported) components of an effective data governance architecture.

> Why do executives continue to underestimate the value of data governance? Because many are still working to appreciate the strategic contribution that data governance makes to corporate performance."

Marinos, George, *The Top 10 Oversights in Data Governance*, Price Waterhouse Coopers, September 2004, accessed at http://www.pwc.com/extweb/pwcpublications.nsf/docid/3B4F18C301B8D2B585256F1100589308.

13. Thompson, Herbert H., and Ford, Richard, *The Insider, Naivety, and Hostility: Security Perfect Storm?*, ACM QUEUE, Vol. 2, No. 4, June 2004, p. 59.

14. GAO, *Technology Assessment: Cybersecurity for Critical Infrastructure Protection*, GAO-04-321, May 2004, p. 24.

15. Trope, Roland L., and Upchurch, Gregory E., CHECKPOINTS IN CYBERSPACE, American Bar Association, 2005, p. 360.

16. The "defense-in-depth" metaphor must be used with caution. When poorly understood or misused in the information security context, it encourages personnel to view security as requiring only static, outer perimeter defenses. However, when correctly understood and applied, "defense-in-depth" requires that security measures be built to assume penetration of outer perimeter defenses, and therefore to necessitate multiple layers of defence and other complementary but diverse measures. Fortress thinking would create a series of concentric walls and in information security a mere layering of firewalls. "Defense-in-depth" when properly applied recognizes that defenses need to be set up against external and internal risks, that they must respond to dynamic threats, and that defenses must fit the active security lifecycle (i.e., protect, detect, respond, and recover).

The dynamic changes in, and hidden nature of, contemporary threats is seldom captured by the fortress metaphor, in large part because what we know about such structures tends to exclude much of their original context of Medieval warfare. Supplying some of that missing context will remind us that castle defenders also had their share of hidden or unseen risks, which is what led to the development of the "moat":

> "Wall tower, barbican and gatehouse enabled the defenders of a castle to keep the enemy at a distance—so long as he remained above ground. The enemy below ground presented a greater problem. Undermining by tunnelling was, in the long run, the most effective way of bringing down a wall or tower. To combat this it was necessary to raise the natural water-table in the vicinity of the castle, so that any tunnel would automatically flood, drowning the miners. This was the original purpose of the castle moat. There were of course, other advantages to be gained from it. A moat made it difficult for an attacker to bring ladders and wooden assault towers close to the castle walls. It provided a supply of water in case of fire. It could even be stocked with fish. But primarily it existed to discourage tunnelling."

Davison, Brian K., THE OBSERVER'S BOOK OF CASTLES, Frederick Warne (Publishers) Ltd., 1979, p. 46.

17. Bishop, Matt, and Frincke, Deborah, *Guarding the Castle Keep: Teaching with the Fortress Metaphor*, IEEE SECURITY & PRIVACY, May/June 2004, p. 69.

18. Ibid.

19. The boundaries between inside and outside a company are also tending to be eroded or made increasingly permeable by introduction of new portable and wireless digital technologies (e.g., PDA's, keychain drives, WiFi, instant messaging, VoIP, peer-to-peer ("P2P")) that can be carelessly or purposefully used to circumvent perimeter defenses. For discussion of wireless risks, see GAO Report, *Information Security: Federal Agencies Need to Improve Controls over Wireless Networks*, GAO-05-383, May 2005, accessed at http://www.gao.gov/new.items/d05383.pdf.

20. "Just about every computer user today is engaged in an evolutionary arms race with virus writers . . . organized criminals, and other individuals attempting to co-opt the Internet for their own purposes. . . . Their attacks are becoming more sophisticated every day, and the

situation will likely become much worse unless we, as defenders, take drastic steps. . . We're faced with adversaries that can potentially deploy attacks faster than we can deploy defenses, even if we use automated update systems."

Somayaji, Anil, *How to Win an Evolutionary Arms Race*, IEEE SE-CURITY & PRIVACY, November/December 2004, p. 70–71.

In addition, monitors of Internet attacks observe that "Hacking has moved from a hobbyist pursuit with a goal of notoriety to a criminal pursuit with a goal of money. Hackers can sell unknown vulnerabilities—'zero-day exploits'—on the black market to criminals who use them to break into computers."

Schneier, Bruce, *Attack Trends 2004 and 2005*, ACM QUEUE, Vol. 3, No. 5, June 2005, pp. 53.

21. Sharp, Sr., Walter Gary, CYBERSPACE AND THE USE OF FORCE, Aegis Research Corporation, 1999, pp. 19, 22, and 25.

See also Schneier, Bruce, *Attack Trends 2004 and 2005*, ACM QUEUE, Vol. 3, No. 5, June 2005, pp. 52–53, observing:

> "Recently there have been worms that use third-party information-gathering techniques, such as Google, for advanced intelligence. . . . We expect to see more attacks against financial institutions, as criminals look for new ways to commit fraud. . . . We also expect to see more politically motivated hacking, whether against countries, companies in 'political' industries (petrochemicals, pharmaceuticals, etc.), or political organizations."

22. Ranum, Marcus J., *Security: The Root of the Problem*, ACM QUEUE, Vol. 2, No. 4, June 2004, p. 45.

23. As Oracle's Chief Security Officer, Mary Ann Davidson, has observed, "I could triple my staff and it would never be enough if developers don't individually accept their own accountability and responsibility." Murray, Sarah, *'Create the correct culture,'* FINANCIAL TIMES FT CORPORATE SECURITY," May 10, 2004, p. 2.

24. Corporate customers are reportedly "fed up with software suppliers releasing unfinished and untested products they have to 'patch and mend,'" in large part because testing and implementing the patches requires considerable time and resources, and is an effort that information technology departments are falling further and further behind in accomplishing. The average internal information technology ("IT") system is reportedly "62 days behind with the latest patches, while the average IT system connected to the internet is 21 days behind." Shill-

ingford, Joia, *Plea to end 'patch and mend,'* FINANCIAL TIMES IT RE-VIEW, October 20, 2004, p. 6.

25. A recent survey of IT professionals revealed frustration with having to comply with legal information security requirements and a begrudging acknowledgment that compliance with such requirements has improved company information security.

> "Two-thirds of those who took part in the survey acknowledged that the wide range of government regulations, such as Sarbanes-Oxley, HIPAA, and GLBA, has affected their company's handling of IT security issues. Among those affected, 62% said they now spend more time complying with those regulations, and less time on activities actually protecting their networks; more than 38% said those regulations have caused them to either divert or delay new IT security projects. But a large majority (66%) acknowledged that compliance with those regulations has, in fact, made their networks more secure."

RedSiren, Press Release, *RedSiren Survey: Computer Security Professionals Grumble That Government Regulations Mean More Work, But Admit They Help Secure Network,* December 22, 2004, accessed at http://biz.yahoo.com/prnews/041222/clw005_1.html.

26. Smedinghoff, Thomas J., *Security & Surveillance: Trends in the Law of Information Security,* BNA INTERNATIONAL WORLD DATA REPORT, Vol. 4, No. 8, August 2004, p. 1.

27. SEC, *Final Rule: Compliance Programs of Investment Companies and Investment Advisers,* RIN 3235-AI77, "Summary," February 5, 2004, accessed at http://www.sec.gov/rules/final/ia-2204.htm.

28. Shearman & Sterling LLP, *Implementing and Reviewing SEC-Mandated Compliance Programs,* March 2005, p. 1.

29. *Citigroup Told To Fix Problems Before Any Mergers,* THE NEW YORK TIMES, March 18, 2005, p. C-4; see also, Franchioni, Michael, *Regulatory Compliance as M&A Obstacle,* PITTSBURGH BUSINESS TIMES, April 15, 2005, accessed at http://pittsburgh.bizjournals.com/pittsburgh/stories/2005/04/18/editorial4.html.

Moreover, the Fed advised Citigroup that "it expected that Citigroup management 'at all levels will devote the necessary attention to implementing its plan fully and effectively and will not undertake significant expansion during the implementation period.'" *Citigroup Told To Fix Problems Before Any Mergers,* THE NEW YORK TIMES, March 18, 2005, p. C-4.

30. The Federal Reserve's Business Continuity Plans distinguish between short-term and long-term disruption, and adopt 48-hours as the cut-off point for short-term disruption. See Federal Reserve Financial Services, *Business Continuity,* accessed at http://www.frbservices.org/BizContinuity/NatCheckPrint.htm. We think the Fed's cut-off time is a useful rule of thumb, but each business should tailor its own plans to the exigencies to which it must respond and the expectations of suppliers, customers and investors. For some companies, such as telecoms, the cut-off point for short-term disruption would probably be less than 12-hours because of the impact such disruptions could cause.

31. As reported in May 2004, "'There's a need to make a cultural leap, to build on a governance programme and turn that into a security programme.' . . . 'Venture capitalists are looking at business continuity as being part of the business plans that they are going to invest in.' . . . But the response within business has yet to reflect this growing investor concern, as abundant research in the past year has shown."
Huband, Mark, *Uneven Levels of Preparedness,* FINANCIAL TIMES FT CORPORATE SECURITY," May 10, 2004, p. 1.

32. Other principles should also be considered. See, for example, the OECD's Generally Accepted Information Security Principles, the Information System Security Association's Generally Accepted Information Security Principles, and the National Institute of Standards and Technology's publications such as AN INTRODUCTION TO COMPUTER SECURITY (SP 800-12), GUIDE FOR DEVELOPING SECURITY PLANS FOR INFORMATION TECHNOLOGY SYSTEMS (SP 800-18), SECURITY GUIDE FOR INTERCONNECTING INFORMATION TECHNOLOGY SYSTEMS (SP 800-47), and WIRELESS NETWORK SECURITY (SP 800–48).

33. The companies that suffered the incidents, dates the incidents were publicly reported, and number of records and/or customers or other persons affected included as of May 2, 2005:

- ChoicePoint; February 15, 2005; 145,000 records, 400,000 customers;
- Bank of America; February 25, 2005; 1.2 million federal government charge cards;
- DSW Shoe Warehouse; March 8, 2005; 1.4 million customers;
- LexisNexis; March 9, 2005; 310,000 customers;
- Boston College; March 17, 2005; 120,000 alumni;
- Polo Ralph Lauren; April 14, 2005; 180,000 customers;
- Ameritrade; April 19, 2005; 200,000 current and former customers;
- Time Warner; May 2, 2005; 600,000 current and former employees.

Without a Trace, THE WALL STREET JOURNAL ONLINE, May 2, 2005, accessed at http://online.wsj.com/documents/info-idtheft0504.html.

34. Trope, Roland, *Directors' Digital Fiduciary Duties*, IEEE SECURITY & PRIVACY, January/February 2005, p. 78.

35. These three features of information assets—confidentiality, integrity, and availability—are considered the features that information security should preserve. See British Standard BS 7799-1:1999, p. 1.

36. We would qualify that statement by noting that, where an organization has implemented a digital signature technology to protect against unauthorized access to its documents, the integrity of such documents can be independently verified by operation of that technology (thereby separating the information asset from its digital lockbox). The organization would be able to determine when documents had been tampered with, but additional effort would be required to identify what changes had been made.

37. Viruses are distinguished by their need for a host program in order to reproduce themselves. They require human intervention usually in order to replicate and distribute themselves from one computer or network to another, e.g., when personnel ignore the well-known cautions against opening unknown file attachments (particularly those that end in ".exe"). Detecting new viruses is a major problem, because anti-virus softwares only protect against known viruses (those that have been released "in the wild" and against which the antivirus software contains an update in order to recognize and quarantine it).

38. Worms differ from viruses in that their creators design them to propagagte through a network (such as the Internet) without human intervention. Each machine they reach becomes a platform at which they replicate themselves and send themselves to other machines. Moreover, where as viruses often damage files on a network, a worm tends to cause a surge in network activity that overloads routers and other network nodes (causing the system to be unable to perform its tasks, i.e., a "denial of service" attack). Detecting new worms is a problem, because by the time a system recognizes the symptoms (such as a flooding of a network by unscheduled activity), the worm has already replicated itself and launched itself against other computers. The defensive measures, in short, often fail to react swiftly enough to contain the damage and prevent its spread to other systems.

39. For a discussion of the legally mandated corporate reporting based on such data, see discussion below of the digital security implications of the Sarbanes-Oxley Act of 2002.

40. Storage of information in any media should be preceded by an assessment of the archival risks and cost-effective means for controlling those risks. Digital media degrade much faster than most organizations realize, and there is a tendency to assume, without investigation, that the media are so resilient they will outlast the need for the data stored on them. When similar errors were made with respect to paper the data might crumble at the touch at the moment one sought to review, search or retrieve it (e.g., paper that was susceptible to decay from acid, such as newsprint, or that was susceptible to decay from light, such as memeograph copies). For a discussion of archival risks and counter-measures for digital storage, see Trope, Roland and Upchurch, Gregory, CHECKPOINTS IN CYBERSPACE, ABA, 2005, Chapter 6 (Information Security), pp. 357–360.

41. "Electronic information, unlike words on paper, is dynamic. The ordinary operation of computers—including the simple act of turning a computer on or off or accessing a particular file—can alter or destroy electronically stored information, and computer systems automatically discard or overwrite data as a part of their routine operation. Computers often automatically create information without the operator's direction or awareness, a feature with no direct counterpart in hard-copy materials. Electronically stored information may be 'deleted' yet continue to exist, but in forms difficult to locate, retrieve, or search. Electronic data, unlike paper, may be incomprehensible when separated from the system that created it."

REPORT OF THE CIVIL RULES ADVISORY COMMITTEE, August 3, 2004, p. 3.

42. Companies should take care not to underestimate the potential scope of records for which they have a broad range of regulatory obligations to retain and preserve in accurate and accessible form. For example, the Occupational Health & Safety Administration ("OSHA") Act contains many provisions that require an employer to create a record if a work-related injury or occupational illness is sustained by an employee and to report certain occurrences. All companies with 10 or more employees are required to maintain employee injury and illness logs unless the company comes within the category of a partially exempt industry, such as finance or insurance.

43. Trope, Roland, *Directors' Digital Fiduciary Duties*, IEEE SECURITY & PRIVACY, January/February 2004, p. 81. [Emphasis added.]

44. Goelzer, Daniel L., *Reporting on Internal Control—The Impact of the Sarbanes-Oxley Act of 2002*, For the Program on Internal Control

Over Financial Reporting at the Spring Meeting of the American Bar Association, Section of Business Law, April 3, 2004, p. 1.

45. PL 107-204, 116 Stat 745.

46. Companies that outsource functions that include a portion of their internal controls or processes that should be governed by those controls must also include in their control assessments an evaluation of the third-party service provider's activities and their effect on such controls. This raises several important and difficult issues that are beyond the scope of this Guide, but which will be increasingly important as companies continue to expand their outsourcing to offshore service providers. Such issues would include:

- determining which outsourced activities must be assessed;
- which outsourced activities must be subject to on-site examinations, direct tests, or audits;
- how to monitor those activities on an on-going basis to ensure timely support for the customer's assessments of its internal controls;
- the allocation of risks between the customer and outsource provider for any errors or breakdowns in controls that may affect the customer's compliance with SOX Section 404;
- in instances where the customer and its auditors do not directly test the outsource service provider's internal controls, whether to rely (and on what conditions to rely) on a Type I, SAS 70 report that the service provider's auditor may provide to demonstrate the effectiveness or quality of the service provider's internal controls; and
- even if the service provider implements ISO 1779 and allows an SAS 70 audit, whether the internal controls will meet the SOX Section 404 requirements.

47. U.S. Security and Exchange Commission, Final Rule on "*Management's Reports on Internal Control Over Financial Reporting and Certification of Disclosure in Exchange Act Periodic Reports*," August 14, 2003, p. 14, accessed at http://www.sec.gov/rules/final/33-8238.htm.

48. Ibid, at p. 20. 17 C.F.R. §229.308(a)(4)(c).

49. 17 C.F.R. §229.308(a)(3).

As the SEC Corporate Finance Staff explains, "When a company identifies a material weakness, and such material weakness has not been remediated prior to its fiscal year-end, it must conclude that its internal control over financial reporting is ineffective."

U.S. Securities and Exchange Commission, Division of Corporation Finance, Office of the Chief Accountant, *Staff Statement on Management's Report on Internal Control Over Financial Reporting*, May 16, 2005, accessed at http://www.sec.gov/info/accountants/stafficreporting. pdf.

50. U.S. Securities and Exchange Commission, Division of Corporation Finance, Office of the Chief Accountant, *Staff Statement on Management's Report on Internal Control Over Financial Reporting*, May 16, 2005, Section E, accessed at http://www.sec.gov/info/accountants/stafficreporting.pdf.

51. Cyber Security Industry Alliance, *Sarbanes-Oxley Act: Implementation of Information Technology and Security Objectives*, December 2004, Section III, p. 9, accessed at https://www.csialliance.org/resources/pdfs/ CSIA_SOX_Report.pdf.

52. PCAOB, Audit Standard No. 2, paragraph 75, quoted in Cyber Security Industry Alliance, *Sarbanes-Oxley Act: Implementation of Information Technology and Security Objectives*, December 2004, Section III, p. 9, accessed at https://www.csialliance.org/resources/pdfs/CSIA_ SOX_Report.pdf.

Audit Standard No. 2 sets the professional standards that govern the independent auditor's attestation and report on the company management's assessment of internal controls over its financial reporting. Auditors are to examine and evaluate such assessment and test it to verify that management's evaluation and conclusions are accurate.

53. U.S. Securities and Exchange Commission, Division of Corporation Finance, Office of the Chief Accountant, *Staff Statement on Management's Report on Internal Control Over Financial Reporting*, May 16, 2005, Section F, accessed at http://www.sec.gov/info/accountants/stafficreporting.pdf.

54. U.S. Securities and Exchange Commission, Division of Corporation Finance, Office of the Chief Accountant, *Staff Statement on Management's Report on Internal Control Over Financial Reporting*, May 16, 2005, accessed at http://www.sec.gov/info/accountants/stafficreporting.pdf.

55. U.S. Securities and Exchange Commission, Division of Corporation Finance, Office of the Chief Accountant, *Staff Statement on Management's Report on Internal Control Over Financial Reporting*, May 16, 2005, Section F, accessed at http://www.sec.gov/info/accountants/stafficreporting.pdf.

56. Final Rule: Management's Reports on Internal Control Over Financial Reporting and Certification of Disclosure in Exchange Act Periodic Reports, 17 CFR PARTS 210, 228, 229, 240, 249, 270, and 274, effective August 14, 2004.

57. Emphasis added.

58. See Office of the Chief Accountant, Division of Corporate Staff, U.S. Securities and Exchange Commission, Management's Report on Internal Control Over Financial Reporting and Disclosure in Exchange Act Periodic Reports Frequently Asked Questions, Question 14 and Answer, accessed at www.sec.gov/info/accountants/controlfaq0604.htm.

59. Pub. L. No. 104-191 (1996).

60. Beaver, Kevin, and Herold, Rebecca, THE PRACTICAL GUIDE TO HIPAA PRIVACY AND SECURITY COMPLIANCE, Auerbach, 2004, p. 3.

61. As mandated under HIPAA, Title II, Subtitle F, Section 261-264.

62. Final Rule, Standards for Privacy of Individually Identifiable Health Information, 45 CFR Parts 160 through 164, December 28, 2000 (Volume 65, Number 250).

63. Final Rule, Health Insurance Reform: Security Standards, 45 CFR Parts 160, 162, and 164, February 20, 2003, (Vol. 68, Number 34).

64. If a covered entity complies with the Privacy Rule, it meets several Security Rule requirements.

65. 45 CFR §164.306(c).

66. 45 CFR §164.306(d)(3)(ii)(B)(1) and (2).

67. 68 FEDERAL REGISTER No. 34, February 20, 2003, at p. 8373.

68. Beaver, Kevin, and Herold, Rebecca, THE PRACTICAL GUIDE TO HIPAA PRIVACY AND SECURITY COMPLIANCE, Auerbach Publications, 2004, p. 163.

69. 45 Code of Federal Regulations, §164.316(b)(1)(ii) and (b)(2)(i), published in 68 FEDERAL REGISTER, No. 34, February 20, 2003, at pp. 8379-8380.

70. Ibid, §164.316(b)(2)(ii).

71. 45 CFR §164.528(a)(1).

72. Except as otherwise provided in the HIPAA regulations, the covered entity must provide the following information concerning each disclosure: date of the disclosure; name of the recipient; address of the recipient; a brief description of the protected health information disclosed; and a brief statement of the purpose of the disclosure that "reasonably informs" the data subject of the basis for the disclosure. If the disclosure was for the purpose of research involving 50 or more persons,

the accounting may (but is not required to) include additional information. See 45 CFR §164.528(b)(2) and (4).

73. 45 CFR §164.528(a)(vi).

74. For example, Section 164.512 identifies several kinds of "permitted disclosure" of protected health information, but, in certain instances, such disclosures may also trigger a requirement (with some exceptions) to notify the individual that their protected health information has been disclosed.

75. HIPAA also applies to PHI and EPHI that may become subject of requests for disclosure during investigations and litigation. See, for example, *Raynor v. St. Vincent's Hospital,* reprinted in NEW YORK LAW JOURNAL, May 17, 2005, p. 18, noting that:

> "Before HIPAA became effective, attorneys for defendants were able to conduct private interviews with plaintiffs' (or their decedents') treating physicians provided that the note of issue had been filed. . . . There was no need for any court involvement in these informal interviews.
>
> HIPAA, however, has changed the legal landscape.
>
> New York courts agree that ex parte interviews are no longer permissible without either (1) an authorization from the patient, (2) a court order or (3) a trial subpoena that assures the doctor that the patent 'received notice of the request or that the [defendant's] attorney secured a protective order.' [case citations]"

76. For further guidance on complying with the Security Rule, see the following NIST publication: Hash, Joan; Bowen, Pauline; Johnson, Arnold; Smith, Carla Dancy; and Steinberg, Daniel I., *An Introductory Resource Guide for Implementing the Health Insurance Portability and Accountability Act (HIPAA)* SECURITY RULE, NIST Special Publication 800-65, March 2005, accessed at http://csrc.nist.gov/publications/nist-pubs/800-66/SP800-66.pdf.

77. 15 USC, Subchapter I, Sec. 6801(a).

78. 15 USC, Subchapter I, Sec. 6801(b).

79. See 16 C.F.R. Part 314, *Standards for Insuring the Security, Confidentiality, Integrity and Protection of Customer Records and Information: FINAL RULE,* effective May 23, 2002.

80. Federal Trade Commission, *Financial Institutions and Customer Data: Complying with the Safeguards Rule,* September 2002, p. 1, accessed at http://www.ftc.gov/bcp/conline/pubs/buspubs/safeguards.htm.

81. Federal Trade Commission, *Standards for Safeguarding Customer Information*, 16 CFR Part 314, FEDERAL REGISTER, vol. 67, no. 100, May 23, 2002, p. 36484 at p. 36489.

82. Federal Trade Commission, *Financial Institutions and Customer Data: Complying with the Safeguards Rule*, September 2002, pp. 1 and 2, accessed at http://www.ftc.gov/bcp/conline/pubs/buspubs/safeguards.htm.

83. Federal Trade Commission, *Standards for Safeguarding Customer Information*, 16 CFR Part 314, FEDERAL REGISTER, vol. 67, no. 100, May 23, 2002, p. 36484 at p. 36490.

84. Ibid.

85. The Board of Governors of the Federal Reserve Board, the Federal Deposit Insurance Corporation, the Office of Comptroller of the Currency, and the Office of Thrift Suspension.

86. 68 FEDERAL REGISTER, No. 155, August 12, 2003, accessed at http://www.mortgagebankers.org/industry/docs/03/68fr47954.pdf.

87. *Interagency Guidance on Response Programs for Unauthorized Access to Customer Information and Customer Notice*, 70 FEDERAL REGISTER, No. 50, pp. 15736–15754, accessed at http://a257.g.akamaitech.net/7/257/2422/01jan20051800/edocket.access.gpo.gov/2005/pdf/05-5980.pdf.

88. In the Guidance, references to the Security Guidelines are "only to the appropriate paragraph number, as these numbers are common to each of the Guidelines." Those paragraph numbers for each agency's Guidelines are: 12 CFR part 30, app. B (OCC); 12 CFR part 208, app. D-2, and part 225, app. F (Board); 12 CFR part 364, app. B (FDIC); and 12 CFR part 570, app. B (OTS).

89. 70 FEDERAL REGISTER, No. 50, March 29, 2005, p. 15752.

90. Additional guidance for developing an organization's incident response program can be found in the following National Institute of Standards and Technology (NIST) guide: Grance, Tim, Kent, Karen, and Kim, Brian, *Computer Security Incident Handling Guide*, NIST Special Publication 800-61, January 2004, accessible at http://csrc.nist.gov/publications/nistpubs/800-61/sp800-61.pdf.

91. The final Guidelines define "sensitive customer information" as follows:

> "A customer's name, address, or telephone number, in conjunction with the customer's social security number, driver's license number, account number, credit or debit card number, or a personal identification number or password that would permit access to the cus-

tomer's account. Sensitive customer information also includes any combination of components of customer information that would allow someone to log onto or access the customer's account, such as user name and password or password and account number."

70 FEDERAL REGISTER, No. 50, March 29, 2005, p. 15752.

92. More specifically, the Guidelines explain:

"When a financial institution becomes aware of an incident of un-authorized access to sensitive customer information, the institution should conduct a reasonable investigation to promptly determine the likelihood that the information has been or will be misused. If the institution determines that misuse of its information about a customer has occurred or is reasonably possible, it should notify the affected customer as soon as possible. Customer notice may be de-layed if an appropriate law enforcement agency determines that no-tification will interfere with a criminal investigation and provides the institution with a written request for the delay. However, the institution should notify its customers as soon as notification will no longer interfere with the investigation."

70 FEDERAL REGISTER, No. 50, p. 15752.

93. Ibid.

94. Federal Trade Commission, Press Release, *FTC Enforces Gramm-Leach-Bliley Act's Safeguards Rule Against Mortgage Companies,* November 16, 2004, accessed at http://www.ftc.gov/opa/2004/11/ns.htm.

95. For a good discussion of measures that GLBA financial institu-tions should consider taking in the event of a security breach, see Dunne, Michael J., and Smith III, Russell F., *Security Has Been Breached: Now What?,* BUSINESS LAW TODAY, November/December 2004, p. 39.

96. See Amendments to the Sentencing Guidelines, Policy State-ments, and Official Commentary, 69 FR 28994-29028, May 19, 2004. The amendments were submitted to Congress on April 30, 2004. The full text of the formal amendments submitted as well as "reader-friendly" versions are available at http://www.ussc.gov/GUIDELIN.HTM.

97. Section 805 of the Sarbanes-Oxley Act of 2002 directed the Com-mission to review and amend the organizational guidelines and related policy statements to ensure that they are sufficient to deter and punish organizational misconduct.

98. Since November 1, 1987, sentences in federal criminal cases have been determined pursuant to the Sentencing Reform Act of 1984 ("SRA") and the U.S. Sentencing Guidelines issued by the United States

Sentencing Commission. Under the previous sentencing regime, judges determined sentences by relying primarily on indeterminate sentencing, i.e., the sentencing judge had discretion to select a sentence within a range bounded by a maximum and minimum sentence. The advent of the Sentencing Guidelines introduced a regime of determinate sentencing in which a legislature or commission would specify precise sentences or set narrow ranges within the broader statutory range, and required the sentencing judge to select a sentence within the prescribed narrow range (with some limited exceptions).

In June 2004, the U.S. Supreme Court held the state of Washington's sentencing guidelines unconstitutional, casting doubt on the constitutionality of the U.S. Sentencing Guidelines. See Blakely v. Washington, 124 S.Ct. 2531, 159 L.Ed. 2d 403, [2004], 2004 WL 1402697 (June 24, 2004). In January 2005, the Supreme Court in United States v. Booker (2005 WL 50108 (U.S. Jan. 12, 2005)) held that the application of the U.S. Sentencing Guidelines could no longer be mandatory because that would conflict with the Sixth Amendment to the U.S. Constitution, and should henceforth be advisory for judges in determining corporate and individual criminal sentences. As noted subsequently by the Second Circuit, "The Supreme Court's decision in Booker significantly altered the sentencing regime that has existed since the Guidelines became effective on November 1, 1987. . . . [A]nd [the decision in Booker] can be expected to have a significant effect on sentencing in federal criminal cases, although perhaps not as drastic an effect as some might suppose." United States v. Crosby, 397 F.3d 103 (2d Cir. 2005) at p. 108 and p. 111. As the Supreme Court made clear in Booker, U.S. District Court judges are now required when determining such sentences to "consult," "consider," and "take account" of the Sentencing Guidelines. As the Second Circuit has explained, "the excision of the mandatory aspect of the Guidelines does not mean that the Guidelines have been discarded. On the contrary, sentencing judges remain under a duty with respect to the Guidelines—not the previously imposed duty to apply the Guidelines, but the continuing duty to 'consider' them, along with the other factors listed in section 3553(a) [of the SRA]." Thus, while applying the Sentencing Guidelines has ceased to be mandatory, judges remain obligated to consider them. What that means in practice will be determined by each of the Circuit Courts of Appeal. For example, the Second Circuit has provided the District Court judges in its jurisdiction express guidance and a caution:

"These principles change the Guidelines from being mandatory to being advisory, but it is important to bear in mind that Booker/Fanfan and section 3553(a) do more than render the Guidelines a body of casual advice, to be consulted or overlooked at the whim of a sentencing judge. Thus, it would be a mistake to think that, after Booker/Fanfan, district judges may return to the sentencing regime that existed before 1987 and exercise unfettered discretion to select any sentence within the applicable statutory maximum and minimum. On the contrary, the Supreme Court expects sentencing judges faithfully to discharge their statutory obligation to 'consider' the Guidelines and all of the other factors listed in section 3553(a)."

397 F.3d 103 at 113–114.

It would, therefore, be prudent for corporations and their counsel to continue to refer to and follow the Sentencing Guidelines when deciding what to include in a company's legal compliance program to ensure that it qualifies as an "effective compliance program" under the Sentencing Guidelines. Moreover, in a January 28, 2005 memorandum, Deputy Attorney General James Comey "urged federal prosecutors to report to the attorney general and to Congress any judges whose sentences fall outside the guidelines range. Prosecutors 'must take all steps necessary to ensure adherence to the sentencing guidelines,' he said in the memo, though the high court rule that such adherence no longer was required. Mr. Comey said in the memo that prosecutors would be required to report to the department all sentences outside the 'appropriate range before imposing an unreasonable sentence.'" Cohen, Laurie P., *Justice Department Is Pressuring Judges on Sentencing Guidelines*, THE WALL STREET JOURNAL, February 2, 2005, p. A4. In light of such pressures by the DoJ, we think it would also be prudent for Directors to remember that the Sentencing Guidelines will be "considered" by all sentencing judges and that Directors should therefore seek to have their organization implement and maintain legal compliance programs that meet the standards for such programs set in the Sentencing Guidelines.

99. More formally, the California Identity Theft Prevention Law, as added to the California Civil Code by Section 4 of California Senate Bill No. 1386.The full text as enacted is available at http://info.sen.ca.gov/pub/01-02/bill/sen/sb_1351-1400/sb_1386_bill_20020926_chaptered.html.

100. Ibid. See *Legislative Counsel's Digest.*

101. See s. 2 adding Section 1798.29(d).

102. See Office of Privacy Protection, Recommended Practices on Notification of Security Breach Involving Personal Information, October 10, 2003, located at http://www.privacy.ca.gov/recommendations/secbreach.pdf.

103. Perez, Evan, and Brooks, Rick, *For Big Vendor of Personal Data, A Theft Lays Bare The Downside*, THE WALL STREET JOURNAL, May 3, 2005, p. A1.

104. Ibid.

A copy of the notice sent by ChoicePoint can be accessed at http://www.choicepoint.com/privacyatchoicepoint/consumers_ca.html.

105. See, for example, Goldberg v. ChoicePoint, Case Number BC 329115, filed in Los Angeles Superior Court on February 18, 2005, claiming violations of business and professional conduct requirements of California law (Sections 17200 and 17203), fraud, and negligent misrepresentation. As of this writing there are four class action suits, all of which have been consolidated in federal court in Los Angeles. The plaintiffs seek monetary, statutory, and punitive damages. Harrington v. Choicepoint, No. 2:05-CV-01294-SJO-JWJ (C.D. Calif.). Baldas, Tresa, *'Fear Factor' Promotes Identity Theft Suits*, NEW YORK LAW JOURNAL, May 12, 2005, p. 5.

106. Baldas, Tresa, *'Fear Factor' Promotes Identity Theft Suits*, NEW YORK LAW JOURNAL, May 12, 2005, p. 5.

107. Testimony of Derek Smith, Chairman and Chief Executive Officer, ChoicePoint, Inc., Before the House Energy and Commerce Committee, Subcommittee on Commerce, Trade and Consumer Protection, March 15, 2005, p. 2.

108. Conkey, Christopher, *Congress Weighs Identity-Theft Remedies*, THE WALL STREET JOURNAL, March 16, 2005, p. A4.

Moreover, as a later report in the same newspaper observed, "Few executives want to risk the kind of public scrutiny that came from the recent security breaches at Reed Elsevier PLC's LexisNexis unit and at ChoicePoint."

McWilliams, Gary, *Identity-Software Sales Are Soaring*, THE WALL STREET JOURNAL, May 12, 2005, p. B4. [Emphases in the original.]

109. Arkansas Senate Bill 1167, an Act to be entitled "An Act to Provide Notice to Consumers of the Disclosure of Their Personal Information; and for Other Purposes," accessed at http://www.arkleg.state.ar.us/ftproot/acts/2005/public/act1526.pdf.

110. Georgia General Assembly, SB 230, a Bill to be entitled an "Act

to amend Chapter 1 of Title 10 of the Official Code of Georgia Annotated," accessed at http://www.legis.state.ga.us/legis/2005_06/pdf/sb230. pdf (however, SB 230 applies only to information brokers and provides *no* penalty for noncompliance by such brokers).

111. Montana House Bill H.B. No. 732, An Act Adopting And Revising Laws To Implement Individual Privacy And To Prevent Identity Theft, signed by Montana's Governor on April 28, 2005, accessed at http://data.opi.state.mt.us/bills/2005/BillHtml/HB0732.htm.

112. North Dakota Senate Bill No. 2251, "an Act relating to requiring disclosure to consumers of a breach in security by businesses maintaining personal information in electronic form," effective June 1, 2005, accessed at http://www.state.nd.us/lr/assembly/59-2005/bill-text/FRBS0500.pdf.

113. Washington Senate Bill 6043, "An Act relating to breaches of security that compromise personal information," effective July 24, 2005, accessed at http://www.leg.wa.gov/pub/billinfo/2005-06/Pdf/Bills/Session%20Law%202005/6043-S.SL.pdf.

114. Punishable by a fine of not less than $50 and not more than $500.

115. The Basel Committee on Banking Supervision is a committee of banking supervisory authorities that was established by the central bank governors of the Group of Ten countries in 1975. It consists of senior representatives of bank supervisory authorities and central banks from Belgium, Canada, France, Germany, Italy, Japan, Luxembourg, the Netherlands, Spain, Sweden, Switzerland, the United Kingdom, and the United States. It usually meets at the Bank for International Settlements in Basel, where its permanent Secretariat is located.

116. See press release "Consensus achieved on Basel II proposals" issued May 11, 2004. Located at: http://www.bis.org/press/p040511.htm.

117. Hargreaves, Deborah, *Banks face heavy IT bill over Basel II*, FINANCIAL TIMES, January 28, 2005, p. 17.

118. Federal Reserve Board Governor Mark W. Olson, *Remarks at the Annual Washington Briefing Conference of the Financial Women's Association*, Washington, D.C., May 15, 2005, accessed at http://www.federalreserve.gov/boarddocs/speeches/2005/20050516/default.htm.

119. "Legal risk" is defined as including, but not limited to, "exposure to fines, penalties, or punitive damages resulting from supervisory actions, as well as private settlements." Basel II: International Convergence of Capital Measurement and Capital Standards: a Revised Framework, page 137, accessed at http://www.bis.org/publ/bcbs107.pdf.

120. Basel II: International Convergence of Capital Measurement and Capital Standards: a Revised Framework, p. 137, accessed at http://www.bis.org/publ/bcbs107.htm.

121. Ibid.

122. Ibid at pp. 141–143.

123. Ibid, p. 142–143.

124. Hargreaves, Deborah, *Banks face heavy IT bill over Basel II*, FINANCIAL TIMES, January 28, 2005, p. 17.

125. *Statement of Thomas J. Curry Director Federal Deposit Insurance Corporation on Basel II: Capital Changes In The U.S. Banking System and the Results of The Impact Study Before the Subcommittee on Financial Institutions and Consumer Credit and Subcommittee on Domestic and International Monetary Policy, Trade, and Technology of The Committee on Financial Services U.S. House of Representatives*, May 11, 2005, FDIC web site, Speeches, Testimony and Articles, pp. 6–7, accessed at http://www.fdic.gov/news/news/speeches/others/spmay1105.html.

126. Ibid, p. 7.

127. Ibid. [Emphasis added.]

128. S. C. 2000, c. 5.

129. *Privacy Act 1988* (Cth), incorporating amendments made to it by the *Privacy Amendment (Private Sector) Act 2000* (Cth).

130. 1998, c. 29

131. Act Of 6 July 2000, Bulletin Of Acts, Orders And Decrees 302, Containing Rules Regarding The Protection Of Personal Data (Dutch Personal Data Protection Act). Unofficial English translation is available at: http://www.ivir.nl/legislation/nl/personaldataprotectionact.html.

132. *Personal Information Protection and Electronic Documents Act*, Schedule 1, Principle 4, Clause 4.7.

133. See Principle 7 of Schedule 1 and associated commentary, of the *Personal information Protection and Electronic Documents Act*.

134. It is important to note that subnational levels of government in other countries, as in the United States, may have enacted data protection laws. The reader is cautioned not to consider the legislative examples cited in this section as being the only ones that might apply in those jurisdictions.

135. *Prepared Statement of the Federal Trade Commission On Protecting Information Security and Preventing Identity Theft, Presented by Commissioner Orson Swindle Before the Subcommittee on Technology, Information Policy, Intergovernmental Relations, and The Census of the*

Committee on Government Reform, United States House of Representatives (September 22, 2004).

136. FTC Commissioner Swindle explains that "The Commission and the courts have defined a deceptive practice as a material representation or omission that is likely to mislead consumers acting reasonably under the circumstances. . . . The Commission also has the authority to challenge practices as unfair if they cause consumers substantial injury that is neither reasonably avoidable nor offset by countervailing benefits."

Prepared Statement of the Federal Trade Commission On Protecting Information Security and Preventing Identity Theft, Presented by Commissioner Orson Swindle Before the Subcommittee on Technology, Information Policy, Intergovernmental Relations, and The Census of the Committee on Government Reform, United States House of Representatives (September 22, 2004), footnote 24.

137. Since the FTC's enforcement actions have focused on companies that permit practices to deviate from published policy concerning privacy and information security, Directors need to ensure that management does not authorize practices that depart from such policies and that management monitors practices closely enough to avert any significant sustained departures. For the same reason, we strongly recommend careful and serious consideration of all risks, including legal risks, associated with proposals that urge companies to "signal their commitment to information security governance by voluntarily posting a statement on their Web site." Corporate Governance Task Force, *Information Security Governance: A Call to Action*, April 2004, p. 9. We advise this caution since any discrepancies between policy and practice will invite FTC scrutiny and prosecution if it finds them to be so significant as to constitute deceptive business practices.

138. *Inquiry Regarding the Entry of Verizon-Maine into the InterLATA Telephone Market*, Docket No. 2000-849, 2003 Me. PUC LEXIS 181, April 30, 2003, pp. 1-32.

139. Ibid. at p. 4.

140. 15 C.F.R. § 734.2(b)(2)(ii).

141. 22 C.F.R. § 120.17(4).

142. 22 C.F.R. § 120.16, definition of "foreign person."

143. See 22 C.F.R. § 120.19 and § 123.9(b) and (c).

Moreover, ITAR § 123.9(b) requires the following statement be an integral part of the bill of lading and the invoice whenever defense articles on the U.S. Munitions List are to be exported:

"These commodities are authorized by the U.S. Government for export only to [country of ultimate destination] for use by [end-user]. They may not be transferred, transshipped on a non-continuous voyage, or otherwise be disposed of in any other country, either in their original form or after being incorporated into other end-items, without the prior written approval of the U.S. Department of State."

144. 69 FEDERAL REGISTER 60829, October 13, 2004.

145. EAR Section 762.2 requires each of the following "original records" to be preserved *for a period of five years* in the form that the person received or prepared them (unless the person meets the conditions for retention instead of an exact image of the original): export control documents; memoranda; notes, correspondence; contracts; invitations to bid; books of account; financial records; and restrictive trade practice or boycott documents and reports.

Similarly, under 22 CFR §122.5(a), all persons required by the ITAR to register with the Directorate of Defense Trade Controls must preserve *for a period of five years* all records relating to the "manufacture, acquisition, and disposition of defense articles."

146. Power, E. Michael, and Trope, Roland, *Averting Security Missteps in Outsourcing*, IEEE SECURITY & PRIVACY, Vol. 3, No. 2, March/April 2005, p. 70 at pp. 72–73.

Discerning and addressing cultural differences are crucial to ensuring the outsource vendor in another country provides the client's required safeguards and meets the client's standards for information security. Overcoming such differences can, of course, be a formidable challenge, as suggested by the insights into India's culture provided by the Indian writer Suketu Mehta:

"India is the Country of the No. That 'no' is your test. You have to get past it. It is India's Great Wall; it keeps out foreign invaders. Pursuing it energetically and vanquishing it is your challenge."

Mehta, Suketu, MAXIMUM CITY, Alfred A. Knopf, 2005, p. 18.

147. 45 CFR §164.528(a)(1).

148. 22 C.F.R. §122.5(a).

149. 17 C.F.R. §240.17a-4(a).

150. 17 C.F.R. §240.17a-4(f)(1)(ii)(a).

151. Scheindlin, Shira A., and Wangkeo, Kanchana, *Electronic Discovery Sanctions In The Twenty-First Century*, 11 MICH. TELECOMM. TECH. L. REV. 71 (2004), at pp. 71 – 72.

152. West v. Goodyear Tire & Rubber Co., 167 F3d 776 (2nd Cir. 1999) at 779.

153. See, for example, Residential Funding Corp. v. DeGeorge Financial Corp., 306 F3d 99 (2d Cir. 2002); Byrnie v. Town of Cromwell, 243 F3d 93 (2d Cir. 2001); and Zubulake V, 2004 U.S. Dist. LEXIS 13574, (S.D.N.Y., 2004). In Zubulake, the Judge imposed a severe penalty for spoliation—she granted the issuance of an adverse inference instruction to the jury.

See also United States of America v. Philip Morris USA Inc., Civil Action No. 99-2496, (D.D.C, 2004), accessed at http://www.dcd.uscourts.gov/99-2496ai.pdf where the District Court in the District of Columbia imposed a monetary sanction in the amount of $2,750,000.

154. Cohen, Adam I., and Lender, David J., ELECTRONIC DISCOVERY: LAW AND PRACTICE, Aspen Publishers, 2004, p. 1-14.

155. We would note that the problem of proper preservation of potentially relevant material is prodigious, and may have little to do with security if the company lacks the ability to determine (across a large enterprise) what information is or is not relevant to the litigation (or government investigation) and thus requires preservation. The preservation, of course, may hinge on the adequacy of the organization's information security.

In the most recent of five UBS Warburg v. Zubulake discovery decisions, District Court Judge Scheindlin gave careful thought and analysis to questions arising out of the duty to preserve. Judge Scheindlin set forth in her opinion what is becoming regarded as a standard for such duties with respect to two main issues—counsel's obligation to ensure that relevant electronically stored information is preserved by giving the client clear instructions to preserve such information and a client's obligations to heed such instructions. As Judge Scheindlin explained:

> "Once a party reasonably anticipates litigation, it must suspend its routine document retention/destruction policy and put in place a 'litigation hold' to ensure the preservation of relevant documents. As a general rule, that 'litigation hold' does not apply to inaccessible backup tapes (e.g., those typically maintained solely for the purpose of disaster recovery), which may continue to be recycled on the schedule set forth in the company's policy. On the other hand, if backup tapes are accessible (i.e., actively used for information retrieval), then such tapes *would* likely be subject to the litigation hold."

"A party's discovery obligations do not end with the implementation of a 'litigation hold' – to the contrary, that's only the beginning. Counsel must oversee compliance with the litigation hold, monitoring the party's efforts to retain and produce the relevant documents. Proper communication between a party and her lawyer will ensure (1) that all relevant information (or at least all sources of relevant information) is discovered, (2) that relevant information is retained on a continuing basis; and (3) that relevant non-privileged material is produced to the opposing party. . . . To do this, counsel must become fully familiar with her client's documents retention policies, as well as the client's data retention architecture. This will invariably involve speaking with information technology personnel, who can explain system-wide backup procedures and the actual (as opposed to theoretical) implementation of the firm's recycling policy. It will also involve communicating with the "key players" in the litigation, in order to understand how they stored information. . . . A lawyer cannot be obliged to monitor her client. . . . At the same time, . . . a party cannot reasonably be trusted to receive the "litigation hold" instruction once and to fully comply with it without the active supervision of counsel." Zubulake V, 2004 U.S. Dist. LEXIS 13574 (S.D.N.Y., 2004) at pp. 24–25 and 29, accessed at http://www.nysd.uscourts.gov/rulings/02cv01243_order_072004.pdf.

These and other issues relating to the "discovery of electronically stored information" are the subject of proposed amendments to the Federal Rules of Practice and Procedure recommended by the Advisory Committee on Federal Rules of Civil Procedure, released for public comment in August 2004.

(Accessible at http://www.uscourts.gov/rules/comment2005/CVAug04.pdf.)

156. See Coleman (Parent) Holdings, Inc. vs. Morgan Stanley & Co., Inc., Case No.: 502003CA005045XXOCAI, *Order On Coleman (Parent) Holdings, Inc.'s Motion for Adverse Inference Instructions,* March 1, 2005, in which the Circuit Court Judge Elizabeth T. Maass, in Palm Beach Florida, granted plaintiff's motion for an adverse inference instruction to the jury that detailed Morgan Stanley's "Destructions of E-Mails" and its "Non-Compliance" with the Court's order. Judge Maass also allowed plaintiff to argue that defendant's "concealment of its role" in the disputed transaction "is evidence of its malice or evil intent, going to the issue of punitive damages," and ruled that defendent Morgan Staley "shall bear the burden of proving to the jury, by the greater weight

of the evidence, that it lacked the knowledge of the Sunbeam fraud and did not aid and abet or conspire with Sunbeam" to commit that fraud. Judge Maass thereby relieved plaintiff of the burden of proving *scienter* to support its claims of fraud against the defendant. *Order* at p. 14.

157. See No. 5:98-cv-2876, slip op. at 72 (N.D. Ohio July 16, 2004), *In Re: Telxon Corporation Securities Litigation*, opinion of Magistrate Judge Hemann, *Report and Recommendation*, July 2, 2004, accessed at https://extranet.prestongates.com/eDiscovery/Files/Report-Recommendation.pdf. As of February 2005, the District Court had not rendered a decision on the Magistrate Judge's recommendation, but as noted in an article co-authored by Judge Scheindlin (who wrote the definitive discovery opinions in Zubulake), "the magistrate's recommended sanction is supported by precedent." Scheindlin, Shira A., and Wangkeo, Kanchana, *Electronic Discovery Sanctions in the Twenty-First Century*, 11 MICH. TELECOM TECH. L. REV. 71 at 88 (2005) accessed at http://www.mttlr.org/voleleven/scheindlin.pdf.

158. Coleman (Parent) Holdings, Inc. v. Morgan Stanley & Co., Inc., Case No.: 502003CA005045XXOCAI, March 1, 2005, p. 10.

See Craig, Susanne, *Age of Discovery: How Morgan Stanley Botched A Big Case by Fumbling Emails*, THE WALL STREET JOURNAL, May 16, 2005, p. 1.

159. See Craig, Susanne, and Scannell, Kara, *Judge's Fraud Ruling Puts Heat On Morgan Stanley, Law Firm*, THE WALL STREET JOURNAL, March 24, 2005, p. 1; Glater, Jonathan D., *Morgan Stanley Gets a Lesson On Lawyers And the Law*, THE NEW YORK TIMES, May 17, 2005, p. C1.

160. Wighton, David, and Silverman, Gary, *Morgan Stanley is told to pay out $600m*, FINANCIAL TIMES, May 17, 2005, p. 1.

161. Wighton, David, *Perelman awarded a further $850m in punitive damages from Morgan Stanley*, FINANCIAL TIMES, May 19, 2005, p. 1.

162. Wighton, David, and Silverman, Gary, *Morgan Stanley is told to pay out $600m*, FINANCIAL TIMES, May 17, 2005, p. 1.

163. See 18 U.S.C. §1512 (b) and (f).

164. Directors should also be keenly aware of the increased risk created by SOX, Section 1512, violation of which is punishable by fines or imprisonment for "not more than 20 years" or both.

165. SOX, Section 1519, accessible at http://news.findlaw.com/hdocs/docs/gwbush/sarbanesoxley072302.pdf.

166. Office of Inspector General of the U.S. Department of Health and Human Services and The American Health Lawyers Association, *Corporate Responsibility and Corporate Compliance: A Resource for Health*

Care Boards of Directors, April 2, 2003, accessed at http://oig.hhs.gov/ fraud/docs/complianceguidance/040203CorpRespRsceGuide.pdf.

167. "[I]t is important to recognize that up to the present, many of the most costly and disruptive cyber events have not been caused by malicious cyber attacks, but instead originated with mundane problems or routine systems mismanagement." U.S. General Accounting Office, *Technology Assessment: Cybersecurity for Critical Infrastructure Protection,* GAO-04-321, May 2004, p. 34.

168. Federal Trade Commission, *Disposal of Consumer Report Information and Records: Final Rule,* 69 Federal Register No. 226, November 24, 2004, p. 68690 at p. 68693.

169. Such responsibility, under SOX, also remains with the subject public company.

170. See General Accounting Office, *Information Security: Information System Controls at the Federal Deposit Insurance Corporation,* May 2004, p. 5.

171. It should be noted that accounts should not be reassigned to incumbents, but should instead be closed and new privileges assigned to the incumbent.

172. Id., p. 15.

173. FFIEC, *Information Security (IT Examination Handbook),* December 2002, p. 79, accessed at www.ffiec.gov/ffiecinfobase/booklets/ information_security/information_security.pdf.

174. WiMAX (an acronym for **W**orldwide **I**nteroperability for **Mi**crowave **Acce**ss), like WiFi, provides wireless connection for broadband Internet service. Whereas WiFi provides single access points for broadband links across the last hundred feet of a network (often within a home or other building), WiMAX was initially envisioned to provide "point-to-multipoint wireless networking . . . for the 'last mile' . . . [and] has a range of up to 30 miles." Chao, Lin, *Preface,* "WiMAX", INTEL TECHNOLOGY JOURNAL, August 20, 2004, p. iii.

175. FDIC, *Guidance on Instant Messaging,* July 21, 2004, accessed at www.fdic.gov/news/financial/2004/fil8404a.html. See also Leavitt, Neal, *Instant Messaging: A New Target for Hackers,* IEEE COMPUTER, Vol. 38, No. 7, July 2005, p. 20.

176. See, GAO, *Information Security: Federal Agencies Need to Improve Control Over Wireless Networks,* GAO-05-383, May 2005, accessed at http://www.gao.gov/new.items/d05383.pdf.

177. See, for example, Avaya, *Security in Converged Networks,* white paper, February 2003, accessed at www1.avaya.com/enterprise/white

paper/msn1841.pdf. See also Kuhn, D. Richard; Walsh, Thomas J.; and Fries, Steffen; NIST, *Security Considerations for Voice Over IP Systems*, SP-800-58, January 2005, accessed at http://csrs.hist.gov/publication-histpub/800-58/SP800-58final.pdf.

178. U.S. Securities and Exchange Commission, Division of Corporation Finance, Office of the Chief Accountant, *Staff Statement on Management's Report on Internal Control Over Financial Reporting*, May 16, 2005, accessed at http://www.sec.gov/info/accountants/stafficreporting .pdf. "Our investigation [in Bergen, Norway] revealed ... company-owned wireless networks with ... no security at all." Hole, Kjell J.; Dyrnes, Erlend; Thorsheim, Per; *Security Wi-Fi Networks*, IEEE COMPUTER, Vol. 38, No. 7, July 2005, pp. 29–30.

179. An excellent resource for checking an organization's incident response policies and procedures is Grance, Tim; Kent, Karen; and Kim, Brian, *Computer Security Incident Handling*, NIST Special Publication 800-61, January 2004, accessed at http://csrc.nist.gov/publications/nist-pubs/800-61/sp800-61.pdf.

180. See Robert Jaques, *Security Tops Network Wish List* at http://www.vnunet.com/news/1156671, last viewed August 17, 2004.

About the Authors

E. Michael Power, a partner in the Ottawa office of Gowling Lafleur Henderson LLP, provides strategic and legal advice to public and private sector clients in the areas of privacy, information technology security, and electronic government. Mr. Power also serves as Gowlings' Chief Privacy Officer. He currently is a member of the National Executive of the Privacy Law Section of the Canadian Bar Association, the Canadian Information Technology Law Association, and the American Bar Association's Cyberspace Law Committee.

Michael Power received his LL.B and M.B.A. from Dalhousie University in 1983. He was admitted to the Nova Scotia Barristers Society in 1984 and the Law Society of Upper Canada in 1991.

Roland L. Trope is a partner at Trope and Schramm LLP, resident in its New York City office, an Adjunct Professor in the Department of Law, United States Military Academy at West Point and in the U.S. Defense Institute for Security Assistance Management, Wright-Patterson Air Force Base, and co-editor of the Digital Protection Department and Privacy Department in the journal *IEEE Security & Privacy*. In his practice he advises on cross-border transactions, export controls, trade sanctions, compliance with privacy and personal data protection regulations, management of data governance and information security, defense procurements, and intellectual property. He co-authored the treatise *Checkpoints in Cyberspace: Best Practices for Averting Liability in Cross-Border Transactions*, published by the American Bar Association in 2005. He is currently a member of the Association of the Bar of the City of New York's Information Technology Committee and the American Bar Association's Cyberspace Law Committee.

Roland Trope received his J.D. from Yale Law School in 1980, a B.A. and M.A. in English Language and Literature from Oxford University in 1972 and 1976, and a B.A. in Political Science from the University of Southern California in 1969. He was admitted to the New York Bar in 1982 and the Minnesota Bar in 1984.